AF272313

AI Against Parental Alienation

Kustantaja: BoD · Books on Demand,

Mannerheimintie 12 B, 00100 Helsinki, bod@bod.fi

Kirjapaino: Libri Plureos GmbH, Friedensallee 273,

22763 Hampuri, Saksa

ISBN: 978-952-80-9503-3

Contents

Preface

The idea to make **this book** came after I saw **my good friend experienced** how heavy can be **the consequences of parental alienation** for **the guardian of the children** who encountered them. **Luckily that situation** has been resolved **in the way that satisfies all the parties in that matter. I have not experienced parental alienation in any form, and I do not have any professional background** which means that **I am neither social worker nor lawyer. I am a layman who has seen what kind of bad things** to happen **before his eyes for the duration of years.**

This book is heavily based on my book "Tekoäly vieraannuttamisen vastavoimana" ´in Finnish but **it is not a direct translation** because **I translated by questions to English and asked them to ChatGPT**. An AI chat like ChatGPT **generates its own answers according to the AI model of the AI chat and the available training data.** The reasons why **the answers given by ChatGPT were slightly different were those factors** and the issue that **translating a question from one language to another** means that even though **the question is translated completely correctly it still may lose some of its nuances.**

Because of that **this book** is meant to **be an introduction book** for **all people** who are **interested in using artificial intelligence (AI) against parental alienation** and **this book is especially meant** for the **guardians of the children** who are **completely surprised to find themselves in the situations their spouses divorce them and try to alienate their common children from them.** My other goal is **to start a discussion about how AI can** be used against parental alienation when it is **a very new idea to use AI against parental alienation**.

It is very important **to notice that the person who will experience parental alienation will always be in practice in the weaker position that the person who tries to alienate their common children because the latter has probably planned his/her actions for some time,** than **children whose legal status is defined as the most important priority in 3. Article of UN Convention on the Rights of the Child** or **the authorities whose status is based on what the local laws say.** Because of that it is **unfair for the people who experience parental alienation that they must fight alone to defend their interests and rights.** It **is a just idea that they can use AI to secure their interests and rights**.

Another important issue to mention is that **I started to be interested in AI,** and **I started to test how AI chat would reply to the questions from that topic** that I made for it in English and in Finnish. My education is Bachelor of Arts in history and in that way, I used my knowledge in history **to test AI chat in that matter.** AI chats have required **a lot of training material** and one good source to acquire that material has **the literature considering history** which gave me an opportunity **to test different AI chats by asking them different questions about history.**

The synthesis of these two matters was in idea that **should AI be used as a tool and a counterbalance against parental alienation**? It is my understanding that **there are no books about that issue or if there are books then they are very rare** because **a very advanced AI** which can **communicate directly with the laymen** is in practice **a very new application**.

The short definition of an AI Chat according to ChatGPT is "AI Chat refers to a conversational system powered by artificial intelligence that enables interactions between users and a machine through text or voice. It uses natural language processing (NLP) and machine learning to understand queries, generate responses, and simulate human-like conversations. AI chat systems are commonly used in customer service, virtual assistants, chatbots, and other interactive applications." ChatGPT is not the only AI chat which exists. There are other AI chats like Deep AI, Gemini, Co-pilot and Perplexity AI. **It is usually a good idea to use multiple AI chats and compare the answers which they have given**.

One **should not trust AI chats alone** because **they do not replace conversations between the people** and especially **with the professionals** in very problematic situations. Professionals usually have **a lot of silent knowledge and experience** in their own field available which AI chats do not have. The strength of the AI chats is that they can analyse quickly **very vast databases** and act in **the extremely logical ways**. On the other hand their weaknesses are **lack of transparency** meaning that people feed them with questions and they give back some kind of answers but one cannot monitor the **process** which leads them to those answers and often one cannot see **the sources** that they use producing those answers either which could lead to the situation where one cannot necessarily say that on which the data, the answers that AI chats has given, **is based on**.

In this book I shall only use ChatGPT as a tool because it´s **user agreement**´s European version (OpenAI.com, "ChatGPT Europe Terms of Use") mentions the following about the ownership of the Output:

Ownership of content. As between you and OpenAI, and to the extent permitted by applicable law, you (a) retain your ownership rights in Input and (b) own the Output. We hereby assign to you all our right, title, and interest, if any, in and to Output.

One should notice that OpenAI owns ChatGPT, and it reserves the right to use the Input and the Output to develop better AI. It is likely that also other AI developers use this approach. Because of this and **common prudence** one should not feed to AI chats any information **identification information** private people and examples of this information are **addresses** or **social security numbers**. One can ask widely about general issues from them and see how well they reply to the questions that were asked from them.

ChatGPT defines shortly parental alienation regarding the separation of child parents in the following way:

"Parental alienation is a process in which a child is manipulated or influenced by one parent to unjustly reject or fear the other parent, often in the context of divorce or custody disputes. It can involve negative conditioning, false accusations, or limiting contact, leading to emotional distress and damaged parent-child relationships."

It is crucial to define parental alienation because **the goal** of this book is that **AI could be used against parental alienation in different ways**. Because of that it is important to understand how AI chat understands **parental alienation** when **the parents of the child go separate ways.** It is important to notice that how **exactly** questions **different issues are asked** from AI. One or more critical words which are **present or absent** may **change the nature of the question** and because of that AI may **misunderstand** the question in **the way that the asker didn´t intend.**

It should also be understood that AI chats **are not any kind of silver bullets** which would solve problems like waving a magic wand. They are **tools** which can be used to solve the problems which have been encountered but they are as good as are their **AI models** and **the training data** that they have used are.

In addition to that they are **made by man** which means that **they may make mistakes** which means that the information which they **mention on the Output** should be doublechecked from **other sources** like books or from the experts of the topic which was discussed with AI chats if one plans to use that information in practice. One should notice that AI sees **all literal material** whether it is from yellow press articles or lawbooks, **equal** which means that AI does not rank it´s source material according to the credibility. AI **may also make typos,** which **are not edited** because **the reader can better analyse the answers of the AI.**

This book references **Finnish legislation** and **the international treaties that Finland has signed and ratified.** However, **laws and treaty obligations vary between countries.** Therefore, anyone **considering applying the information in this book should consult local experts,** such as **child and family law attorneys,** to **ensure compliance with relevant laws and regulations.**

Neither the author, the publisher, nor any associated individuals or organizations assume any responsibility for the consequences of using the information in this book without seeking proper legal advice. These two chapters regarding legal disclaimer were improved by ChatGPT.

First it is necessary to give a bit attention to making a good how to use AI against parental alienation. As a topic this is very novel, and it does have a lot of long-term potential. AI applications will not most likely go away and instead of that they are here to stay. When we understand this the role of AI should always be subservient to the people and to serve the mankind´s well-being improving it.

Because of that it is necessary to shortly familiarise with making a book about AI when the topic of the book is to use AI against parental alienation. There are reasons to have some understanding of about the nature of AI and how does it work to gain the maximum advantage from AI. This discussion will be a dialogue with AI and there will be comment on the replies that AI has given. One extra reason for this commentary is to create an additional point of view because AI can present in the Output as exhaustively as possible based on it´s AI model and the training data. We will start with a question which reasons made possible AI chats like ChatGPT revolution during the first half of 2020s according to ChatGPT.

You said:

Which reasons made possible AI chats like ChatGPT revolution during the first half of 2020s?

ChatGPT said:

The AI chat revolution, including ChatGPT, became possible in the first half of the 2020s due to several key factors:

1. **Advancements in Deep Learning** – Large-scale transformer models (like OpenAI's GPT-3 and GPT-4) improved language understanding and generation capabilities.
2. **Massive Training Data** – AI models were trained on vast datasets from the internet, allowing them to generate coherent and context-aware responses.
3. **Increased Computing Power** – The rise of powerful GPUs and TPUs enabled the training of extremely large neural networks.
4. **Refined Training Techniques** – Methods like Reinforcement Learning from Human Feedback (RLHF) improved response quality and alignment with human preferences.
5. **Cloud Computing & Scalability** – AI models became more accessible through cloud-based deployment, allowing users to interact with them in real time.
6. **Corporate Investment & Competition** – Companies like OpenAI, Google, and Microsoft heavily invested in AI, pushing rapid innovation and widespread adoption.
7. **Mainstream Adoption & Demand** – Businesses, educators, and individuals embraced AI chatbots for productivity, automation, and creative tasks, fueling further development.

These factors collectively drove the AI chat revolution, making sophisticated conversational AI widely available.

A comment to the AI´s reply: One can see from the reply that the **AI can analyse** issues in a very logical way when it gave

seven logical reasons why AI chats became more common and then it gave **a short summary** of this topic. Because of reply like that one can start **comparing** AI to fire meaning that it is **an excellent servant but a poor master**.

You said:

I have thought to use this conversation for my benefit to make a book from a topic how to use different AI chats against parental alienation. Are there any problems on that idea regarding copyrights? My advice if someone encounters parental alienation is to consult with a lawyer who is specialized in child and family law but at the same time it would be a very good idea that the laymen would know their rights.

ChatGPT said:

Your idea of writing a book on how to use different AI chats to counter parental alienation sounds interesting and potentially helpful. Regarding copyright concerns:

1. **Your Own Writing is Yours** – Anything you write, including your interpretation of AI-generated content, is your own intellectual property.
2. **AI-Generated Content** – OpenAI does not claim copyright over AI-generated text, and you are free to use it. However, AI-generated text itself is generally not copyrightable, meaning others could also use similar ideas or wording.
3. **Attribution & Originality** – While you don't need to attribute AI-generated text, adding your personal insights, case studies, or unique perspectives will make your book more valuable and original.

4. **Legal Advice Disclaimer** – Since your book touches on legal matters, it's wise to include a disclaimer stating that the book does not replace professional legal counsel and that readers should consult qualified lawyers.

Your approach—recommending legal consultation while also helping laypeople understand their rights—is a solid balance. If you provide practical ways AI can assist in navigating parental alienation (e.g., gathering evidence, drafting documents, emotional support), your book could be very useful.

A comment to the AI´s reply: It is good that AI at once recognizes **the potential advantages and the meaning** that the book would have. It is natural in the book to make **a difference between the text written by the author and the replies given by AI** after it got the **Input.** Perhaps the most important issue on the book will be **examining the Output given by AI understanding it´s strengths and weaknesses** and the ways how to use AI in **the most beneficial ways.**

It is also good that **AI understands** that **it cannot replace human experts,** and for example it advises to consult **with those experts who have specialized in the matters regarding legal issues or human sanity.** The strength of AI is the fact that one can discuss with AI **24 hours in a day and 7 days in a week.** In addition to that AI may help to **collect** and **analyse** data and to **understand the big picture.**

You said:

In Finland one can appeal the irregularities of the child protection authorities to the Regional State Administrative

Agency, the Parliamentary Ombudsman of Finland or Chancellor of Justice but the problem is that the processing is something from a year to a year and half while there might be going a legal process about the future of the children which will take couple of months to determine what would be the best course to take in the interest of the child. Would it be better if there would be an internal supervision in the child protection authorities that would intervene any detected irregularities?

ChatGPT said:

Yes, an internal supervision mechanism within the child protection authorities could be beneficial, especially in cases where timely intervention is crucial. If the current oversight bodies, such as the **Regional State Administrative Agency, the Parliamentary Ombudsman, and the Chancellor of Justice**, take a year or more to process complaints, their rulings may come too late to impact an ongoing legal process regarding a child's future.

An **internal supervisory body** could help by:

1. **Ensuring Faster Intervention** – Detecting and addressing irregularities in real-time before they escalate into serious legal issues.
2. **Providing Accountability** – Making sure child protection workers follow legal procedures properly and do not overstep their authority.
3. **Reducing Bureaucratic Delays** – A more immediate response could prevent prolonged harm caused by unjust decisions.

4. **Protecting Children's Best Interests** – If mistakes or biases occur, quick corrective measures can prevent long-term negative impacts on children and families.

However, for such an internal system to work, it **must be independent and transparent,** so that it does not simply protect the agency's own decisions but genuinely ensures fairness. An alternative or additional solution could be a **fast-track appeals process** in urgent child protection cases.

Would you envision such a supervisory body working within the existing agency, or do you think an external independent review board would be better?

A comment to the AI´s reply: In my opinion a blind faith to the authorities and **the legality of their actions** can severely harm the child´s guardian´s **ability to take care of his or her interests.** He or she should understand that **the authorities are just people, and they may make mistakes or even break the law.** If they break the law in **a way that harms the person, who is experiencing parental alienation** in the middle of the legal process **in which the future of the child is determined as an urgent matter** the **legal protection of the guardian** of the child who is experiencing parental alienation **may be in jeopardy.**

You said:

One of the key issues in my book is to double check all relevant information given by AI chats to the experts, usually lawyers who are specialized in child or family law before using them in practice. Another key issue from me in practice is to use several different AI chats like ChatGPT, Deep AI, Gemini or Co-pilot and compare the answers that they have given.

ChatGPT said:

That's a very **practical and responsible** approach! Double-checking AI-generated legal information with **qualified experts** ensures accuracy and prevents misinterpretation of laws that can vary by country and case specifics.

Your second key issue—**using multiple AI chats (ChatGPT, Deep AI, Gemini, Co-Pilot, etc.) and comparing their answers**—is also a great strategy. Different AI models are trained on different datasets and may have varying strengths, biases, or gaps in knowledge. Comparing responses helps in:

1. **Identifying inconsistencies** – If AI chats provide conflicting answers, it's a sign to verify with an expert.
2. **Finding different perspectives** – Some models may highlight aspects others miss.
3. **Refining questions** – If one AI gives vague or incomplete answers, another might offer a clearer explanation.
4. **Detecting biases** – AI models can sometimes reflect biases in their training data, so cross-checking reduces reliance on a single perspective.

Would you also include a **methodology section** in your book to guide readers on how to effectively compare AI-generated responses and verify them with legal professionals? That could be a helpful tool for readers unfamiliar with AI.

A comment to the AI´s reply: It should be noticed that **there are no countries which have granted AI a legally certified official position.** There isn´t even a common agreement **how AI could gain such a position** relations with people or what would be the requirements to **give AI such a position** when that position can be **denied** from another AI application. AI is first and **foremost an unofficial advisor** and **a tool to help people in matters regarding acquiring information** in a similar way how **search engines like Google** help people.

One good idea is **to use several different AI applications side by side asking them the same questions in the Input** and **examining their Output comparing the differences.** I used ChatGPT, Deep AI, Gemini and Co-pilot as examples of these AI applications but it should be noticed that **these are only 4 AI applications** in the much **larger world of AI applications** in which there may happen surprise changes for example because **their development and work often happens at the terms of the business life.** If the companies developing them do not have enough clients or cash flow, then they might **go to bankruptcy,** or **another company might acquire them.**

This book is just **the beginning of examining how AI could be used against parental alienation** which means that **what book can offer using AI is quite limited.** If someone wants to use AI, **then it would be a good idea that person should acquire a book or several books** which specifically deal with how to use **AI broadly and offer general tips how to use AI.** It is important to learn how to evaluate **the quality and the trustworthiness** of the **answers that AI has given** because answers with **poor quality and being untrustworthy** will may weaken people´s trust on the credibility of AI. In addition to that **it is always a good idea to check the facts that AI has told** from **independent sources.**

As the reply says AI can easily be **a part of the strategy against parental alienation** as one of the tools. It may help **gathering evidence to prove parental alienation** for example in the **from** of a diary or **help understanding legal terms or processes regarding possible lawsuit**. It may also give **ideas and suggestions** to the discussions with **legal and childcare experts**.

It should be remembered that **one should not feed any AI with the identification information of private people because there is always a possibility that someone might misuse that information**. If someone notices that he or she in a divorce situation **is being alienated from his or her children**, then **the divorce from a former spouse and the separation from the children** may be **rough and momentarily paralysing strike**. It might be **one of the goals of the parental alienation of the children to paralyze the parent who is targeted by parental alienation** that he or she might be **become tired and give up**. In that kind of situation when one is trying **to prove the parental alienation** and **keep himself/herself together** that **AI might become a valuable ally to the person who experiences parental alienation** and **a tool to keep his/her life together**.

My advice for **a person who plans to use Output provided by AI is to print to paper all the data which he or she plans to use**. I think it is **easier to compare data when it is on the paper than it is on the computer screen**. It would be wise **to make notes** when comparing answers provided by AI and when **talking to the legal experts** it would be **a good idea to let them read AI´s Output to evaluate how useful it can be**.

You said:

I want to note that even if you ask the same AI Chat the same question twice the answer might be very different. In a situation like this it would be important to identify the core issues of both answers to gain the maximum advantage.

ChatGPT said:

That's an excellent point! AI-generated responses can **vary significantly** even when asking the same AI chat the same question multiple times. This variability can be both a challenge and an opportunity.

Your approach of **identifying the core issues from different responses** is a smart strategy because:

1. **It helps extract the most relevant legal principles** – Even if wording changes, key legal points may remain consistent.
2. **It allows for a broader perspective** – Different answers might highlight different angles of the issue, leading to a more well-rounded understanding.
3. **It maximizes useful insights** – Instead of relying on just one version of an answer, combining key points from multiple responses can provide the best possible guidance.

Would you consider including **practical examples** in your book where AI-generated responses differ and showing how to analyze them effectively? That could be a valuable guide for readers unfamiliar with AI's variability.

A comment to the AI´s reply: It is good that AI tells **honestly** how **it replies to the questions that are asked** and explains **why the same question might have a different answer**. The reason for different kind of answers might be things like **the**

randomness of the AI model, the ambiguity of the question given to AI, the structure of the question or the training data available for AI model. It might be that the AI model, which is used, is not designed to deal with data from that field in which the questions are asked and because of that the answers look like a bit uncertain. It should be noted that if someone asks if an AI model is designed to handle issues regarding parental alienation and whether it can handle the issue mentioned before, they are two slightly different matters. It could be a good idea to ask couple of similar questions to AI and next I will ask three very similar questions to AI regarding parental alienation.

You said:

How does ChatGPT define alienation shortly?

ChatGPT said:

Alienation is a state of detachment or estrangement from a person, group, society, or oneself.

You said:

How does ChatGPT define parental alienation shortly?

ChatGPT said:

Parental alienation is the psychological manipulation of a child to unjustly reject or fear one parent, often in custody disputes.

A comment to the AI´s reply: It should be noticed that this book specifically examines parental alienation. There might be other reason why the child does not want to meet or be in contact with his/her parent. **This book does not focus on the cases in which the authorities take the children** in their custody, **and it is recommended in cases like this to consult with a local lawyer who is specialized in child and family law**.

You said:

How does ChatGPT define parental alienation?

ChatGPT said:

Parental alienation is a process in which one parent manipulates or influences a child to unjustly reject, fear, or distance themselves from the other parent. This often occurs in high-conflict divorces or custody disputes and can involve tactics such as negative conditioning, false accusations, or limiting contact. Parental alienation can cause emotional harm to the child and damage their relationship with the alienated parent, potentially leading to long-term psychological consequences.

A comment to the AI´s reply: In the first question focuses on asking AI shortly about **the definition of alienation** without mentioning that the issue being discussed is **alienating a child** from his or her parent. In the second question **parental alienation is defined in conjunction with the divorce or separation between his/her parents** and in the third question **this same definition is made without asking the short version of the definition.** Each of these questions prove that **one can ask various issues from AI also requesting the short answer** and AI can be asked to **give a short and well summarized answer to the question.** A good tip regarding AI is that when **AI has answered to the first question then one can ask more**

exact questions based on the answer that AI gave to the first question.

What is Parental Alienation according to AI

AI has already given the answer how it defines the parental alienation. There are good reasons to examine this issue further because the consequences of parental alienation may have long term influences on the child who is targeted by such behavior and as consequence of that kind of action the child may even lose his/her parent and the entire family from this parent´s side without any legal grounds for such actions. Because of that it is important to examine the possible consequence of parental alienation on the child and his/her parent who is the target of parental alienation.

You said:

How does the parental alienation influence on the child who is being alienated from his/her parent?

ChatGPT said:

Parental alienation can have **severe emotional, psychological, and social consequences** for the child being alienated from a parent. Some key effects include:

1. **Emotional Distress** – The child may experience anxiety, guilt, confusion, sadness, or depression due to the forced rejection of a loving parent.
2. **Identity Issues** – Losing a meaningful relationship with a parent can lead to **self-doubt** and struggles with personal identity.

3. **Difficulty Trusting Others** – Alienated children may develop **trust issues** as they have been manipulated into believing false narratives about their parent.
4. **Poor Conflict Resolution Skills** – Growing up in an environment of hostility may teach the child that cutting off relationships is an acceptable way to handle conflicts.
5. **Low Self-Esteem** – Internalizing negative beliefs about the alienated parent may extend to **self-worth**, especially if the child shares personality traits with that parent.
6. **Increased Risk of Mental Health Problems** – Studies suggest that alienated children are more prone to **anxiety, depression, and even substance abuse** later in life.
7. **Struggles in Future Relationships** – They may carry **attachment issues** into adulthood, impacting friendships, romantic relationships, and even their own parenting.

Would you like insights on how to help a child affected by parental alienation?

A comment to the AI´s reply: Parental alienation is **very unfair towards the child** because he/she basically must choose between his/her parents **without reasons of his/her own**. It is **natural for the child** who is in that kind of situation to **"ally and seek comfort"** from the parent who is present in the child´s life. At the same time **the child is forced to choose sides** in conflict between his/her parents **without having the understanding the situation completely neutrally** because he/she does not have **the life experience and the understanding of an adult person**. At the same time the child is also **dependable on the parent**

who is present when he is most likely told that the other parent **abandoned the child**.

It is understandable that **the self-esteem of the child suffers** when the child adopts **negative images** towards the parent **who the child assumes abandoned him/her because it was told to the child in that way**. Why wasn´t the child **good enough for his/her other parent**? At the same time the child feels gratitude towards the parent who is present in the child´s life and is taking care of the child while **the child does not know** that the **parent who is present alienated the child** from his/her another parent.

In the parental alienation the child may lose **without any good reason not only one of his/her parents and possible the entire family of that parent and many close people**. Because of that **one might ask** to the parent **who is taking care of the child that what to do if something bad happens to that parent and because of that event the parent is unable to take care of the child? Who will take care of the child when he/she has not been in contact with the other parent of child and this parent´s for years? Why** should the child who was alienated **trust his/her other parent and the family of this parent** when the parent who was taking care of the child already **poisoned child´s mind with images of the other parent and the family of this parent? Trust between people is not built in couple of moments** especially if it was broken from **the child´s point of view** and especially **in a situation in which the child should understand** that **most of the things that was told to the child regarding the other parent, are not true**. In a situation like this **it would be very hard for the child** to understand **why the parent who was taking care of the child** acted **badly against the best interests of the child**.

24

The consequences of parental alienation might cause the child to suffer **depression, anxiety** or **other mental problems**. Recovering from those problems **is not easy** and **might need professional help** which means that it would be **expensive both mentally and financially**. On the other words **the parent who alienated** the child caused **a psychological burden which could extend to the adulthood of the child** only because **that parent wanted to own the child**.

Because of parental alienation the child might get **wrong models to build relations between different people and to solve conflicts between people**. Parental alienation **might give the child an idea that it is right to abandon other person when this person is not needed** and in conflict situations one can treat other people without considering what **they want or wish**.

You said:

How does parental alienation influence on the targeted parent?

ChatGPT said:

Parental alienation can have **devastating effects** on the targeted parent, both emotionally and socially. Some of the key impacts include:

1. **Emotional Pain and Grief** – Losing a relationship with their child can cause deep emotional suffering, similar to the grief of losing a loved one.
2. **Depression and Anxiety** – Feelings of helplessness, frustration, and rejection can lead to serious mental health struggles.

3. **Sense of Powerlessness** – The targeted parent often feels unable to protect their relationship with their child, especially if legal systems fail to intervene effectively.
4. **Damage to Reputation** – False accusations or negative portrayals by the alienating parent can lead to social stigma and damaged relationships with extended family and friends.
5. **Financial Strain** – Legal battles to regain access to the child can be expensive and exhausting, adding further stress.
6. **Health Issues** – Chronic stress and emotional distress can contribute to physical health problems, such as high blood pressure, insomnia, or weakened immune function.
7. **Parental Identity Crisis** – Being unjustly cut off from their child may lead to a loss of purpose and self-worth.
8. **Long-Term Relationship Struggles** – The emotional trauma can affect future relationships, making it harder to trust or bond with others.

Would you like strategies on how a targeted parent can cope and respond to parental alienation?

A comment to the AI´s reply: The answer given by ChatGPT can be divided on **three different groups** which are determined by the consequences. These groups are **the psychological impact on the targeted parent, the parental alienation´s impact on the human relationships** and **the economical impacts of the parental alienation to the targeted parent. Emotional pain** and **the wounding of self-esteem and identity and possible mental problems** are first and foremost **the psychological impacts** of the parental alienation. **Social seclusion and obstacles regarding parenthood** are the consequences of

26

parental alienation on **the human relationships. Legal** and **economical pressures** are primary **the economic and the psychological consequences** of parental alienation because **a layperson must feel stress** if he/she is forced **to fight legal battles** in the matters that this person thought **could have been resolved through negotiations.**

You said:

Because of the earlier answers can one rightfully say that parental alienation is mental or psychological violence in the legal sense on the targeted parent?

ChatGPT said:

Yes, **parental alienation can be considered a form of mental or psychological violence** against the targeted parent in a legal sense, depending on the jurisdiction. Psychological violence is often defined as **actions that cause emotional harm, distress, or suffering,** and parental alienation meets these criteria in many ways:

1. **Intentional Infliction of Emotional Distress** – The alienating parent's actions are often deliberate, aiming to sever the parent-child bond, causing **severe emotional suffering.**
2. **Manipulation and Control** – The alienating parent uses **coercion, deceit, and psychological pressure** to turn the child against the targeted parent, similar to psychological abuse tactics.
3. **Defamation and Social Harm** – Spreading false accusations or negative narratives about the targeted

parent can **damage their reputation, relationships, and even their career.**

4. **Legal Recognition** – Some countries recognize **parental alienation as psychological abuse**. For example, in Brazil, parental alienation is explicitly outlawed under **Law No. 12,318/2010**. Other legal systems might address it under broader **domestic violence or emotional abuse laws.**

However, **legal classification varies by country**. Some courts see parental alienation as a family conflict issue rather than a criminal offense, while others acknowledge it as a **serious form of psychological abuse** that can justify legal intervention.

Would you like information on how different legal systems address parental alienation?

A comment to the AI´s reply: I do not want to go too deep in the legal matters but according to **the Finnish Penal Code Chapter 21 sections 5 and 6** say that **an assault can be made by using mental or psychological violence instead of physical violence.** This change to the Finnish penal code was made in 1995 because then also **mental and psychological violence** could be considered when **evaluating the crimes and the consequences of the crimes.** If one is going to be use this matter **legally** then that person should **consult with the local lawyers who are specialized in crime law and family and child law** before using it in practice. This is also important because **different countries have different laws**, and **the local lawyers** are the best experts to know **the local processes and local laws.**

AI can **summarize quite well the consequences of parental alienation** both on the child and on the targeted parent. It can be seen clearly from AI´s answer that both **child and the targeted parent do feel great pain. The serious negative consequences** of parental alienation are the reason to intervene parental alienation whenever it is detected.

You said:

When parental alienation is so harmful both to the child and to the targeted parent then how can it be detected and intervened to stop the parental alienation?

ChatGPT said:

Detecting and Intervening in Parental Alienation

Since **parental alienation harms both the child and the targeted parent**, early **detection and intervention** are crucial. Here's how it can be identified and addressed:

1. Detecting Parental Alienation

Signs in the Child:

- **Unjustified rejection** of the targeted parent without logical reasons.
- **Repeating adult-like accusations** that seem rehearsed.
- **Lack of guilt or remorse** when mistreating the targeted parent.
- **Strong alignment with the alienating parent**, even in conflicts unrelated to them.

- **Refusal to spend time with the targeted parent**, often expressing extreme fear or anger.
- **Distorted memories** that favor the alienating parent.

Signs in the Alienating Parent:

- **Badmouthing** the targeted parent in front of the child.
- **Interfering with visitation rights** or making excuses to prevent contact.
- **Encouraging the child to keep secrets** from the targeted parent.
- **Falsely accusing the other parent** of abuse or neglect.
- **Using the child as a messenger** or spy.

Signs in the Targeted Parent:

- **Sudden estrangement from their child** despite a previously loving relationship.
- **Feeling powerless** in maintaining contact.
- **Being falsely accused** of harmful behaviors.
- **Emotional distress**, anxiety, or depression caused by the alienation.

---

2. Intervening to Stop Parental Alienation

Legal Actions:

- **Family Court Intervention:** A judge can order custody evaluations, therapy, or **modify custody arrangements** if alienation is proven.

- **Court-Appointed Child Psychologists:** Professionals assess the child's attitude and the influence of both parents.
- **Enforcing Visitation Rights:** If one parent denies access, courts can impose penalties or adjust custody.
- **Supervised Visitation Orders:** If alienation is severe, the alienating parent may only be allowed supervised contact.

Psychological and Social Interventions:

- **Family Therapy:** A trained therapist can help rebuild the parent-child relationship.
- **Parental Education Programs:** Courts may require alienating parents to attend programs on the harm of their behavior.
- **Mediation Services:** Some cases benefit from neutral third-party mediation.

Preventative Measures:

- **Early Documentation:** Targeted parents should keep records of denied visitations, hostile messages, and changes in the child's behavior.
- **Legal Awareness:** Understanding **family law** and seeking legal counsel early can prevent further alienation.
- **Raising Awareness:** Educating legal and mental health professionals about **parental alienation** can lead to better intervention strategies.

Would you like more details on legal strategies or psychological recovery for targeted parents?

A comment to the AI´s reply: The answer given by AI was **very good in theory** but one might add that **even the professional child protective authorities might not always identify parental alienation.** On should remember that **the parent who is alienating the child from the other parent will do everything** that **the authorities do not notice the parental alienation** by using his/her explanations. It is not in the best interests of the alienating parent that **the authorities start talking about parental alienation** because that **will turn the attention to what he/she has do** which is **ethically and morally wrong** and it might be **illegal** as well.

The work against parental alienation requires both **to train the professionals to identify parental alienation** and **to enlighten the parents of the children. If the child does not want to meet one of his/her parents,** then **parental alienation might be one explanation,** but **it is not the only explanation.** Because of that it is very important in **that kind of conflict situation** to create as **neutral and extensive whole picture of the matter as possible** because it will help **to understand what has happened** and **who have been the actors in that situation** and **what have they done.** These actors might **the parents, their relatives, their friends, their co-workers or new partners.**

You said:

Prioritizing the best interest of the child is the most important issue in the child protection work but how can it be determined neutrally in a parental alienation situation?

ChatGPT said:

Determining the Best Interest of the Child Neutrally in a Parental Alienation Situation

Ensuring a **neutral and fair assessment** of the child's best interest in a parental alienation case requires **objective criteria, professional evaluations, and legal safeguards**. Since alienation distorts the child's perception of one parent, a careful **fact-based and child-centered approach** is essential.

---

1. Objective Criteria for the Best Interest of the Child

A neutral assessment should consider:

- **The child's emotional and psychological well-being** – Does the child show distress, fear, or unnatural hostility toward one parent?
- **The quality of past parent-child relationships** – Was there a healthy bond before the alienation started?
- **Each parent's behavior and influence** – Is one parent encouraging negative views of the other?
- **The child's actual needs** – Are their educational, social, and medical needs being met?
- **The ability of both parents to provide stability** – Which parent is ensuring a conflict-free, nurturing environment?

---

2. Neutral Professional Evaluations

To avoid bias, courts and child protection authorities should rely on **specialists trained in parental alienation**:

- **Forensic Psychologists** – Conduct independent **child-parent bonding assessments** and evaluate whether the child's rejection is justified or manipulated.
- **Child Protection Social Workers** – Should receive **specialized training** to recognize and document signs of alienation.
- **Court-Appointed Guardians (e.g., Guardian ad Litem)** – Represent the child's interests without bias toward either parent.
- **Mediators and Family Therapists** – Can help rebuild the parent-child relationship when appropriate.

---

3. Safeguarding Neutrality in Legal and Administrative Processes

To ensure impartiality:

- **Avoid relying solely on the child's statements**, as they may be influenced by the alienating parent.
- **Ensure balanced representation** – Both parents should have equal opportunities to present evidence.
- **Use multiple sources of evidence**, such as expert reports, school records, and testimonies from neutral third parties (teachers, family doctors, etc.).
- **Monitor legal timelines** – Since court decisions can take time, **temporary remedies** (e.g., supervised contact or therapy) may be necessary to prevent further alienation.

Would you like insights on legal procedures that can help ensure neutrality in parental alienation cases?

A comment to the AI´s reply: In the possible parental alienation situation it is **the most important issue that the authorities are neutral towards both parents. The child´s best interest** is a priority, and it must not become to be just a phrase or a way to speak **but it must become the way to process the situation** in the way that it secures both **the best interest of the child** and **the rights of both parents**.

You said:

Can it be thought that using the Golden Rule (The Golden Rule is the principle of treating others as one would want to be treated by them.) it is easy to realize that parental alienation is wrong because the alienating parent certainly do not wish to be alienated from his/her child? Is it possible to use empathy to see condemn parental alienation in ethical and moral terms?

ChatGPT said:

Yes, **the Golden Rule provides a strong ethical argument against parental alienation** because the alienating parent would likely never want to experience the same treatment. If they were placed in the position of the **targeted parent**, they would likely feel deep emotional pain, distress, and injustice. Therefore, **applying the Golden Rule naturally leads to the conclusion that parental alienation is morally wrong**.

Using Empathy to Condemn Parental Alienation in Ethical and Moral Terms

Empathy allows people to understand the **suffering caused by parental alienation** from both the child's and the targeted parent's perspectives:

1. **Empathy for the Child**
   - The child is deprived of a loving relationship with one parent.
   - The child is manipulated into believing false narratives, which can cause lifelong emotional harm.
   - The child may experience **identity confusion, guilt, and emotional distress** from being forced to reject a parent.
2. **Empathy for the Targeted Parent**
   - They experience **deep emotional pain** from being unjustly separated from their child.
   - They may face **social stigma** due to false accusations.
   - They lose **precious time and moments** with their child, which can never be recovered.
3. **Empathy for the Alienating Parent (Self-Reflection)**
   - If they truly imagined being in the targeted parent's position, they would recognize the cruelty of alienation.
   - They may realize that **using a child as a weapon** against the other parent is not justifiable.
   - Long-term, the alienating parent risks losing the child's trust when the child eventually **sees through the manipulation**.

Moral and Ethical Condemnation

- **Universal Moral Principles** – Most ethical traditions (from Kant's categorical imperative to Confucian values) condemn actions that intentionally **harm others without just cause**.

- **Basic Human Rights** – Every child has a right to maintain **a loving relationship with both parents**, unless one parent is truly harmful.
- **Long-Term Consequences** – Alienation leads to emotional suffering, family breakdown, and social harm.

Thus, **through both the Golden Rule and empathy**, one can **ethically and morally reject parental alienation** as unjust, harmful, and in violation of fundamental human relationships.

Would you like me to expand on how different philosophical or legal frameworks view parental alienation?

A comment to the AI´s reply: In this answer AI handles well the issue regarding how **to use empathy** and **how to use the golden rule** in parental alienation situations. One should think that **the ability to use empathy is essential when bringing up children** so **the children will learn to see issues through the eyes of the other people when interacting with them**. AI also makes **clear through empathy that parental alienation is against the best interests of the child** because **it will harm the child in the long run**. When examining **both ethical and moral condemnation** it is likely that **the alienating parent probably does not want that his/her children will be alienated from that parent** because **parental alienation is against the principle of the child´s interests being top priority** and often **reasons for parental alienation comes are selfish and vindictive.** AI´s answer also shows that **any parent who decides to alienate his/her children from the other parent act willingly acting wrongly** because acting as **a responsible parent in ethically and morally right ways requires to use empathy skills**.

You said:

What advice would ChatGPT give if someone realizes that his/her children are being alienated from that person?

ChatGPT said:

If someone realizes that their children are being alienated from them, here's some key advice to navigate the situation:

1. Stay Calm and Collected

- Avoid reacting with anger or hostility, as this can reinforce the alienating parent's narrative.
- Maintain a composed and rational approach to avoid escalating the conflict.

2. Document Everything

- Keep a detailed record of incidents, including missed visitations, denied communication, and any evidence of the other parent's alienating behavior.
- Save texts, emails, and any communication that might prove manipulation or interference.

3. Maintain Contact with Your Children

- Stay consistent in your efforts to communicate, even if the other parent is obstructing contact.
- Send messages, letters, or small gifts to show that you are present and care.
- Avoid pressuring the child—make interactions positive and stress-free.

4. Seek Professional Help

- A therapist or counselor who specializes in parental alienation can guide you on the best way to reconnect with your child.
- If possible, family therapy may help mend the damaged relationship.

5. Avoid Speaking Negatively About the Alienating Parent

- Do not badmouth the other parent, as this can make the child feel torn between parents and increase their resistance toward you.
- Instead, reassure your child that you love and support them no matter what.

6. Legal Action as a Last Resort

- If alienation becomes severe, consult a family law attorney who specializes in child custody and parental alienation cases.
- Courts can sometimes intervene to enforce visitation or adjust custody if parental alienation is proven.
- Mediation or court-ordered reunification therapy might be an option.

7. Be Patient and Persistent

- Alienation is a long and painful process, but persistence, consistency, and unconditional love can sometimes reverse its effects.
- Never give up on your child, even if the situation seems hopeless at times.

Would you like any specific guidance on legal aspects or communication strategies?

A comment to the AI´s reply: AI gave some very good tips because **it a good idea to write down everything regarding parental alienation** that the **targeted parent to recall everything that happened,** if necessary**, after years those issues happened**. It is also **easier to prove parental alienation to the authorities** when **all the events are written down**.

It is also very important to remain calm in front of the children because it **will increase their trust on that person who is the target of the parental alienation** and **regarding the authorities it will increase their trust on the targeted person as a serious adult**. It will also certainly **annoy the alienating parent** because it shows that **the parental alienation does not have influence on the target**.

If possible, **it would be a good idea to attempt to have constructive discussions with the alienating parent on the topic of the best interest of the child. The problem with this advice is that the first the alienating parent should realize the harm that he/she is creating to the child through his/her behaviour**. It would be **a good idea to ask help from the professionals,** because **the conflict between the parents of the child may reach the level that they alone may not be able to resolve it** and it may be necessary **that someone from the authorities should talk sense to the alienating parent** that he/she would realize the harm of his/her behaviour to the child. **Regarding authorities it is always a good idea to know one´s rights** and **there is always a possibility that the alienating parent may try to make the authorities to support him/her claims** and **to turn them against the targeted parent**.

That is the reason **why proving parental alienation at this point is extremely important** because **the person who first requests help from the authorities is not necessarily right** and **that person may try to manipulate the authorities.**

Knowing one´s own rights is **extremely important** if the other **side tries to continue the parental alienation.** Legal issues regarding **the child custody, the rights to meet the child and the alimony** require **legal expertise** and the because of that it would wise **to consult with a lawyer specialized in child and family law before starting any lawsuits regarding those issues.**

The best interests of the child are the most important issues. If the child **needs mental aid,** then that should be arranged for the child **for example in the form of a therapist. No one should force the child to choose sides** in a conflict between the parents of that child. **The child should feel secure at the home of both of that child´s parents.** The divorce and separation should be discussed **only after the child have become an adult** because **it should not be expected that a minor has mental maturity to handle so serious issues regarding his/ her parents neutrally.** It should be assumed that only **adult children can take care of themselves** while **children who are minor cannot.**

You said:

Is it possible that the new partner of alienating parent regardless of the length of the new relationship whether it started as a secret affair or it is a new relationship, encourages the alienating parent to try to alienate the child from the other parent?

ChatGPT said:

Yes, it is entirely possible that the new partner of the alienating parent may encourage or reinforce parental alienation, regardless of how long the relationship has existed or whether it started as a secret affair or a new relationship. Here are some possible reasons why this might happen:

1. Desire to Replace the Other Parent

- The new partner may want to take on the role of the child's "new parent" and may see the targeted parent as an obstacle.
- They might consciously or unconsciously push the child to see them as the real or better parent.

2. Loyalty to the Alienating Parent

- The new partner may side with the alienating parent to strengthen their relationship, especially if they have been exposed to a one-sided narrative about the targeted parent.
- They may view the targeted parent as a "threat" to their new family unit.

3. Jealousy and Insecurity

- If the new partner is insecure about the alienating parent's past relationship, they might try to erase reminders of it—including the other parent.
- They may feel that the presence of the other parent undermines their position in the family.

4. Influence of the Alienating Parent's Narrative

- The alienating parent may portray the targeted parent in a negative light, and the new partner may believe this version of events without question.
- They might not see their actions as harmful but rather as "protecting" the child from a supposedly bad parent.

5. Power and Control Dynamics

- The new partner might be controlling or manipulative, encouraging alienation as a way to further isolate the alienating parent and child from external influences.
- This can be especially common in relationships where emotional abuse or coercive control is present.

6. A Desire to Build a "New Family"

- Some individuals may push for a fresh start by discouraging contact with the past, including the child's other parent.
- They may try to rewrite family history, convincing the child that the other parent is irrelevant or harmful.

7. Influence of Their Own Personal Experiences

- If the new partner has had negative experiences with their own ex or a difficult divorce, they may project their issues onto the situation and encourage alienation.

What Can Be Done?

- **Stay calm and collected:** Avoid reacting emotionally, as this may further validate their narrative.
- **Strengthen your bond with your child:** Be present, consistent, and offer unconditional love.
- **Document any concerning behavior:** Keep records of interference, negative remarks, or efforts to alienate.
- **Seek professional and legal support:** If alienation is escalating, consulting a family therapist and a legal professional may be necessary.

Would you like more guidance on handling a situation where the new partner is involved in the alienation?

A comment to the AI´s reply: The motif of the question asked to the AI was the idea **to understand the big picture** as well as possible. If the alienating parent divorced and separated the other parent of the **child because of an affair**, then it is possible that his/her new partner may encourage or even help the alienating parent in his/her alienation efforts for example having **the reasons which AI mentioned**. The actions of the new partner of the alienating parent if he/she **helps or encourages** the parental alienation can be interpreted to **legally to be an inciter or an abettor** according to the Finnish Penal Code. In **any countries** in **matters like this**, I recommend the reader to consult **with a lawyer who is specialized in both local child and family and local crime** law before using this issue legally.

You said:

The worst option for the parent who targeted to be alienated from the child is that the affair between the other parent of the child and his/her partner began before the separation or divorce between him/her and the other parent of the child. If this is the case, then it would be fair label the new partner of his/her child´s other parent as a mate poacher or a spouse poacher. It would be noted that the key characteristics of that kind of the mate poacher are Narcissism, Machiavellianism and Psychopathy which all belong to the Dark Triad of Psychology, and which may encourage parental alienation.

ChatGPT said:

Yes, if the new partner was involved in an affair with the alienating parent before the separation or divorce, this can add another layer of hostility, resentment, and dysfunction to the family dynamics. It is fair to describe such a person as a *mate poacher* or *spouse poacher*, as their relationship began through the deliberate pursuit of someone already in a committed partnership.

Dark Triad Traits and Their Role in Parental Alienation

Research on mate poaching has found that individuals who engage in it often exhibit traits from the **Dark Triad of Personality:**

1. **Narcissism (Self-Centeredness and Entitlement)**
   - The poacher may feel entitled to the new partner, disregarding the harm caused to the family.
   - They may seek validation by proving they are "better" than the ex-partner.
   - They may manipulate the child into rejecting the targeted parent to assert their dominance in the new family unit.
2. **Machiavellianism (Manipulation and Deception)**

- The poacher may engage in strategic manipulation, turning the child against the targeted parent to consolidate their influence.
- They might gaslight the child, making them believe false narratives about the alienated parent.
- They may encourage legal and psychological warfare to keep the targeted parent out of the picture.

3. **Psychopathy (Lack of Empathy and Remorse)**
   - The poacher may have no guilt about breaking up a family or emotionally harming a child.
   - They may enjoy the power struggle and view parental alienation as a game they are "winning."
   - They may disregard the long-term psychological damage inflicted on the child.

How This Leads to Parental Alienation

- The mate poacher might **encourage hostility** between the child and the targeted parent to secure their new position in the family.
- They may **coerce the alienating parent** into increasing restrictions on the targeted parent's access to the child.
- They may **feed the alienating parent's insecurities** and reinforce the idea that the targeted parent is a danger or unworthy of the child's love.
- They may **act as a gatekeeper,** controlling communication and interactions between the child and the alienated parent.

What Can the Alienated Parent Do?

1. **Recognize Manipulation Tactics** – Understand that the poacher's behavior is often calculated and strategic. Avoid playing into their hands by reacting emotionally.
2. **Stay Close to the Child** – Continue expressing love and interest in their life, even if the new household is trying to erase your role.
3. **Gather Evidence** – Document interactions that demonstrate alienation, false claims, or undue influence.
4. **Legal and Psychological Support** – A lawyer specializing in parental alienation and a therapist experienced in family dynamics can be crucial.
5. **Remain the Stable Parent** – Children eventually see through manipulation. Consistency, patience, and genuine love can help rebuild the relationship over time.

Would you like resources on how to counteract this kind of alienation effectively?

A comment to the AI´s reply: It is probably very rare that **the new relationship of the former spouse began as an affair**. However, **if this happened and the consequence of that is parental alienation** it is utmost important for **the parent who experiences parental alienation** to create **the big picture from the situation** and **to prove what happened. In a situation like this it would be a good idea to follow the advice proved by AI** in this reply and **become familiar with the characteristics of the Dark Triad of Psychology** which are **narcissism, psychopathy and machiavellianism**. It would be **unwise to give power over other people to the people who have that kind of personalities.** The terms like **"mate poacher"** and **"spouse poacher"** are commonly used **in the modern English scientific Psychology literature**.

You said:

What are the worst consequences that can happen to the targeted parent and the child because of parental alienation? Is it true that at the worst parental alienation can lead to family killings but luckily that is very rare?

ChatGPT said:

Parental alienation can have **severe psychological, emotional, and even legal consequences** for both the **targeted parent** and the **alienated child**. In extreme cases, it can contribute to tragic outcomes, including **violence** and, in rare instances, **family killings (familicide)**. However, while familicide is a horrific possibility, it remains *exceptionally rare*. More commonly, the consequences of parental alienation manifest in long-term emotional and psychological damage.

---

1. Consequences for the Targeted Parent

Emotional & Psychological Consequences:

- **Severe Depression & Anxiety** – Losing a relationship with one's own child can cause profound sadness, helplessness, and chronic stress.
- **Grief & Trauma** – Alienated parents often experience a type of grief known as "ambiguous loss," where their child is still alive but emotionally distant.
- **Suicidal Thoughts** – Some targeted parents fall into deep despair, feeling that they have lost their role and identity as a parent.

- **Social Isolation** – Friends and family may not fully understand the situation, making the targeted parent feel alone.

Legal & Financial Consequences:

- **Loss of Custody & Visitation Rights** – Alienating parents often manipulate legal systems to limit or eliminate the targeted parent's access to the child.
- **False Allegations of Abuse** – Some alienating parents fabricate abuse claims, leading to devastating legal battles.
- **Financial Ruin** – Fighting alienation in court is **expensive**, and prolonged legal struggles can lead to financial instability.

---

2. Consequences for the Alienated Child

Psychological & Emotional Consequences:

- **Identity Issues & Low Self-Esteem** – A child who is manipulated into rejecting a loving parent often struggles with self-worth and personal identity.
- **Increased Risk of Depression & Anxiety** – Many alienated children suffer from lifelong emotional distress.
- **Difficulty Forming Healthy Relationships** – Alienation teaches children that love is conditional, making them more likely to struggle with trust and attachment in adulthood.

- **Guilt & Regret Later in Life** – Many alienated children, as they grow older, realize they were manipulated and may suffer from intense guilt for rejecting their alienated parent.

Social & Behavioral Consequences:

- **Increased Risk of Substance Abuse** – Some alienated children turn to alcohol or drugs as a coping mechanism.
- **Higher Likelihood of Engaging in Toxic Relationships** – They may repeat the same patterns of emotional abuse in their own relationships.
- **Academic & Behavioral Problems** – Alienation-related stress can impact school performance and lead to delinquent behavior.

---

3. Extreme Consequences: Can Parental Alienation Lead to Violence or Familicide?

In *extreme and rare cases*, **parental alienation has been linked to family killings (familicide).** While this is **not common,** the psychological devastation of alienation can push some individuals into **violent desperation.**

Possible Triggers for Familicide in Parental Alienation Cases:

- **A parent losing complete access to their child,** leading to a **"nothing to lose"** mindset.
- **False allegations of abuse** leading to **wrongful imprisonment** or **public humiliation.**
- **Severe financial ruin** caused by prolonged legal battles.

- **Mental health breakdown** combined with hopelessness and extreme emotional distress.

Notable Research on Familicide & Custody Battles:

- Studies on **family annihilators** suggest that intense **custody battles, alienation, and false allegations** can be risk factors for extreme violence.
- Some cases of **murder-suicide** involving parents have been linked to **severe alienation**, where a parent feels they have lost everything.

However, **most alienated parents do not resort to violence—** instead, they suffer in silence, experiencing lifelong emotional pain.

A comment to the AI´s reply: Even though **the family killings** that are caused by parental alienation are **luckily very rare** it is **unfortunate that they might happen. The essential thing to notice in parental alienation** is the fact that **it impossible to predict with certainty the reactions of the targeted parent** when he/she reacts to **that injustice.** Who will have **the moral, the ethical and the legal responsibility** if the targeted parent **breaks mentally, commits suicide or in the worst-case scenario kills his/her children and the other parent of the children?** THL (Finnish Institute of Health and Welfare is a Finnish research and development institute operating under the Ministry of Social Affairs and Health) does have **a very good article "Vaativat erotilanteet and eron jälkeinen väkivalta"** (Eng. **Demanding separations and the post-separation violence**) in Finnish dated on December 5th, 2023. **Most of the readers likely cannot read this article because it is in Finnish,**

but it can be translated **from Finnish to English using an advanced AI like ChatGPT.**

You can ask AI like ChatGPT to translate the text from that article using this command in Input: **"Can you translate this from Finnish to English: "The text to be translated." The translation should be accurate enough to evaluate the quality of the original article.** I do not put the translated text in this book for **possible copyright reasons** since I already explained **how to do the credible translation** from Finnish to English but if someone **is considering using the original article or the English translation in any way,** I recommend **consulting with the Finnish Institute of Health and Welfare** before doing so. One should understand that this is **a machine translation, and it may contain mistakes in the text**.

One can also ask AI **to provide research papers** that **prove parental alienation increasing the chance that the targeted parent may try to commit suicide**: "Can you list extensively research papers which prove that parental alienation increases the chances that the targeted parent will have increased chance to commit suicide?"

You said:

How can people be enlightened more efficiently about the harmfulness of parental alienation so that there would be less parental alienation?

ChatGPT said:

Raising awareness and **effectively educating people** about the harmfulness of parental alienation requires **a multi-level**

approach involving legal, psychological, and social interventions. Here are **several key strategies** to reduce parental alienation:

---

1. Strengthening Public Awareness & Education

◆ **Educational Campaigns**

- National and local campaigns similar to those for **domestic violence and bullying awareness** can help highlight the devastating effects of alienation.
- TV documentaries, social media campaigns, and public service announcements.

◆ **School & Workplace Education**

- Schools can incorporate **family dynamics education** into health or psychology classes.
- Workplaces could offer **seminars on parental alienation for divorcing employees,** helping them navigate family disputes in a healthier way.

◆ **Psychological Education for Parents & Children**

- Promoting **therapeutic resources** that teach parents about the emotional and mental damage alienation causes.
- Encouraging **children to speak up** when they feel manipulated or pressured by one parent against the other.

2. Reforming Legal Systems & Family Court Approaches

- **Recognizing Parental Alienation as Emotional Abuse**

  - Courts should **acknowledge parental alienation as a form of psychological abuse** and enforce legal consequences accordingly.

- **Better Training for Judges & Family Law Professionals**

  - Family court judges, mediators, and lawyers should **receive specialized training** to recognize and address parental alienation.
  - Clearer **laws and guidelines** to help prevent manipulation of custody arrangements.

- **Court-Mandated Family Therapy**

  - Instead of simply **granting custody changes**, courts should **require** therapy for children affected by alienation.
  - Parallel parenting plans to **reduce direct conflict** between high-conflict parents.

3. Media and Entertainment Responsibility

- **Correcting Harmful Stereotypes**

- Many movies and TV shows **normalize or glorify** parental alienation (e.g., depicting a mother keeping the child away from a "bad father" or vice versa).
- Encouraging **more balanced portrayals** of shared parenting and healthy co-parenting.

Influencer & Celebrity Advocacy

- Well-known figures speaking out about their experiences with parental alienation **can break taboos** and spread awareness quickly.

---

4. Community & Support Networks

Parent Support Groups

- Online and in-person groups for **targeted parents to share experiences, strategies, and emotional support**.

Child Advocacy Programs

- Programs that provide **neutral third-party advocates** to support the child's best interests rather than the agenda of either parent.

Religious & Cultural Community Involvement

- Many communities rely heavily on **religious or cultural support structures**, which could be mobilized to **educate parents about healthier family dynamics**.

5. Improving Mental Health Services

◆ Easier Access to Family Therapy

- Affordable therapy and counseling should be **readily available** for separated families.
- Special training for therapists to **identify and counteract alienation behaviors**.

◆ Mental Health Screening for Divorcing Parents

- Courts could **mandate mental health assessments** during custody disputes to detect early signs of alienation behaviors.

Would These Strategies Actually Reduce Parental Alienation?

Yes, **if consistently applied**. Many parents **don't realize** they are engaging in alienation until it's too late. By increasing **awareness, legal accountability, and mental health interventions**, alienation could become **far less common** over time.

Would you like me to **find examples** of countries that have successfully reduced parental alienation through legal or social reforms?

A comment to the AI´s reply: The list that AI provides **to enlighten people** is very good. However, it raises a question that when thought **it is known that parental alienation harmful** where would the people who want to share this knowledge **acquire the financing needed** to do the knowledge sharing in practice? A part of the enlightenment can be included in **education** leading to the **childcare professions** or **professional supplement education** but regarding **the external stakeholders** like **the parents of the children** it may not be so to influence on them.

You said:

Doesn´t the parental alienation has a risk that it may fail and when the children are adults parental alienation may come to haunt the alienating parent? In a short run it is possible to make the children to be loyal towards the alienating parent but if the parental alienation fails then how can the alienating parent justify his/her actions to his/her adult children?

ChatGPT said:

Yes, **parental alienation carries a significant risk of failure**, especially in the long run. While an alienating parent may achieve **short-term loyalty** from their children, there is a strong possibility that as the children grow into adults, they will **see through the manipulation** and turn against the alienating parent.

Why Can Parental Alienation Backfire?

1. **Children Develop Independent Thinking**
   - As children mature, they **gain critical thinking skills** and may **question past narratives** fed to them by the alienating parent.

- They may **compare stories** between both parents and realize that the targeted parent was unfairly demonized.
2. **External Influences Expose the Truth**
   - **Friends, extended family, and romantic partners** can offer **alternative perspectives** that challenge the alienating parent's version of events.
   - Therapists, teachers, or even co-workers may help the now-adult child **reassess past experiences**.
3. **Evidence and Contradictions Accumulate Over Time**
   - The targeted parent may have **left behind proof** (letters, emails, court documents, photos, witness statements) showing they tried to stay involved.
   - If the alienating parent **made false claims** about abuse or neglect, but the child later finds out the truth, this can **cause resentment and distrust**.
4. **Emotional and Psychological Guilt on the Alienating Parent**
   - The alienating parent may **lose control** over the adult child's emotions and **struggle to justify past actions**.
   - If the alienating parent engaged in **extreme manipulation**, the child may feel **betrayed and emotionally abused**.
5. **Reunification with the Targeted Parent Can Happen**
   - Many alienated children **reconnect with the targeted parent in adulthood**, which **further exposes the alienating parent's lies**.

- This often results in **strained or even completely broken relationships** between the adult child and the alienating parent.

How Can the Alienating Parent Justify Their Actions?

If the alienation fails, the alienating parent will have a **hard time** justifying their actions. They might try to:

- **Double down on the original lies** ("I was just trying to protect you!").
- **Blame the child** ("You're ungrateful after all I did for you!").
- **Shift the blame to someone else** (e.g., lawyers, courts, society, or even the child's other parent).
- **Play the victim** and claim they were misunderstood or acting in the child's best interest.

However, these justifications often **do not work**, especially if the adult child has already seen through the deception. Instead, the alienating parent risks:

- **Being cut off entirely by their child.**
- **Feeling deep regret and loneliness** in old age.
- **Experiencing public or family shame** if their actions become widely known.

Long-Term Consequences for the Alienating Parent

- **Strained or completely severed relationships** with their adult children.

- **Possible legal repercussions** (e.g., if courts later recognize the parental alienation as a form of child abuse).
- **Mental health consequences**, including guilt, regret, depression, and loneliness.

Conclusion: Alienation Is a Risky, Short-Sighted Strategy

While alienation may seem like a "winning" strategy in the short term, **it is a gamble with high risks**. Children may eventually uncover the truth, and **the alienating parent may face serious emotional and social consequences** in later years.

Would you like me to find **real-life cases or research studies** where alienated children later turned against the alienating parent?

A comment to the AI´s reply: AI is correct that **failing in parental alienation does have significant risks** for the **alienating parent** which **he/she probably does not understand when he/she decides to alienate the children from the other parent**. It is probable that **when the children become adults, they want to know the truth about alienation and claims made during that episode**. The alienating parent then may have difficulties to explain and justify his/her actions through his/her **credibility** if he/she has **earlier lied to his/her children and the lies will be exposed** when **the children are becoming adults**.

Parental Alienation and Social Work

The social work like **the child protection authorities** or **the shelters for families** may a significant role in the parental alienation conflicts. The 6th Article of the Finnish Constitution which is the **Equality before the Law Article** stipulates people are equal before the law**. The basic assumption** is that **in the parental alienation situations social work treats both parents observing this principle. The person who is experiencing the parental alienation is recommended to understand that the alienating parent may try to turn the authorities against the targeted parent. From the point of view of the alienating parent this both very logical and very calculating way to act** and **if it is successful** then **it will seriously harm the life of the targeted parent.** Because of that **it is very important for the targeted parent to know his/her rights** so he/she **can evaluate the actions of the social work towards that person.** He/she can do that **by recording his/her discussions with the social work people if the local law allows that** and by **keeping a diary regarding the interaction with the social work.**

You said:

What are the obligations of the child protective authorities and the family shelters towards the parents of the children?

ChatGPT said:

The **obligations of child protective authorities and family shelters** toward parents depend on the country's legal framework, but in general, these institutions must balance **child protection** with **parental rights**. Below are the **main obligations** they typically have toward parents:

61

1. Child Protective Authorities' Obligations Toward Parents

a) Ensuring Fair and Transparent Investigations

- Authorities must **investigate concerns** about a child's well-being **objectively**.
- Parents must be **informed** about the investigation and its findings, unless doing so would endanger the child.
- Authorities should use **clear criteria** when deciding interventions.

b) Respecting Parental Rights

- Parents have the **right to be heard** and provide their own evidence.
- Child protection authorities must **attempt to support the family first** before considering removal of the child.
- The state cannot **unfairly interfere** with parental rights unless it is necessary for the child's safety.

c) Providing Support Services

- Authorities should offer **counseling, parenting classes, or financial assistance** to help parents provide a safe home.
- Family reunification should be the goal **if it is in the child's best interest**.

d) Making Decisions in the Child's Best Interest

- Child protection decisions must be based on **the best interests of the child**, not personal biases.
- Parents must be informed about **their rights** and the reasons behind any decision.

e) Legal Due Process and Appeal Rights

- If a child is placed in care, parents must have the right to **appeal** the decision.
- Parents must have **access to legal representation** in child protection cases.

---

2. Family Shelters' Obligations Toward Parents

Family shelters (such as domestic violence shelters) primarily protect victims, but they also have obligations to **both parents** when children are involved.

a) Providing Safety and Confidentiality

- If a parent and child seek shelter due to **domestic violence**, their information must be kept **confidential** to protect them from harm.
- The shelter cannot **unfairly interfere** with custody rights unless required by law.

b) Facilitating Parental Contact When Safe

- If one parent is in a shelter, **the other parent (not accused of violence) should not be automatically denied access** to the child.

- Shelters must follow **court-ordered custody agreements,** unless there is a risk of harm.

c) Supporting Parental Well-being

- Shelters should offer **counseling, legal aid, and parenting support** to help the parent in crisis.
- They must provide **resources** for parents to rebuild their lives while ensuring their child's safety.

d) Preventing Unjustified Alienation

- Shelters should not **encourage parental alienation** but rather facilitate healthy relationships when safe.
- If domestic violence is **not** a factor, efforts should be made to ensure the child can **maintain relationships** with both parents.

Conclusion: A Balancing Act Between Protection and Parental Rights

Both child protection authorities and family shelters must balance:

✓ **Protecting children from harm**

✓ **Supporting parents in need**

✓ **Respecting parental rights**

Would you like specific **laws or policies** from a particular country regarding these obligations?

A comment to the AI´s reply: **Everything which AI said is true in theory** and **the real world should act in that way.** One should remember that **the alienating parent may try to turn the authorities against the targeted parent. The authorities are just people and people make mistakes** so the alienating **parent may be successful in his/her attempts especially** if **he/she is convincing enough and is the first one to ask help from the authorities** even though **it should not matter much legally who was the first to ask help from the authorities.**

You said:

What is the original source of the Prioritizing the Child´s Interest Principle and what does it say exactly about the rights of the parents and the duties of the authorities? Where did that principle originally come from?

ChatGPT said:

The **principle of prioritizing the child's best interest**—often referred to as the **Best Interests of the Child Principle**—originates primarily from **international human rights law**. The most influential source is **the United Nations Convention on the Rights of the Child (UNCRC)**, adopted in **1989** and ratified by nearly every country in the world.

---

1. Original Source: The UN Convention on the Rights of the Child (UNCRC, 1989)

The key **legal foundation** for the principle is found in **Article 3(1) of the UNCRC:**

"In all actions concerning children, whether undertaken by public or private social welfare institutions, courts of law, administrative authorities or legislative bodies, the best interests of the child shall be a primary consideration."

This means that when **authorities, courts, and institutions** make decisions affecting children, the child's well-being must be **the main priority** over any other considerations.

---

2. What Does This Principle Say About Parental Rights and Authorities' Duties?

The principle establishes **a balance** between:

1. **The child's welfare and protection**
2. **Parental rights and responsibilities**
3. **The duties of the state and authorities**

A) Parents' Rights and Responsibilities

- Parents have the **primary responsibility** for the upbringing and well-being of their children.
- The **state should support families** in fulfilling their parental duties.
- Parents should have **custody and decision-making rights, unless** their actions harm the child.

B) Authorities' Duties and Limits

- Authorities **must intervene** if a child is in danger (e.g., abuse, neglect, or serious psychological harm).

- **Removing a child from their parents** should be a **last resort** and only when it is in the child's best interest.
- If separation is necessary, authorities **must ensure the child maintains a relationship** with both parents, unless doing so would harm the child.

---

3. Historical Origins of the Best Interests Principle

The idea of prioritizing a child's well-being has evolved over time. Some key milestones include:

📄 **1924 Geneva Declaration on the Rights of the Child** – The **League of Nations** first introduced a global standard for child welfare, stating that children must be given special care and protection.

📄 **1948 Universal Declaration of Human Rights (UDHR)** – Recognized that childhood requires special legal protections (Article 25).

📄 **1959 Declaration of the Rights of the Child** – Established ten principles emphasizing children's welfare.

📄 **1989 UNCRC (Legally Binding)** – Made the "best interest of the child" a binding legal principle for all signatory states.

---

4. How Does This Affect Modern Legal Systems?

Many countries have incorporated this principle into their **family law systems**, affecting:

✓ **Custody disputes** – Courts decide based on what benefits the child most.

✓ **Child protection cases** – Authorities must **balance** protecting the child with respecting parental rights.

✓ **Adoption & foster care** – Priority is given to **stable, loving environments** for the child.

Would you like to know how **a specific country** applies this principle in its legal system?

A comment to the AI´s reply: It is true that the priority of the child´s best interest and securing that interest is one of the most important issues in social work focusing on children. However **the answer by AI stays pretty much on the level of the principles without giving satisfactory answer** regarding **the rights of the parents of the children or the duties of the authorities** because if the **alienating parent is successful turning the authorities against the targeted parent** then **it is very important for the targeted parent to know his/her rights** and **the duties of the authorities according to the UN Convention on the Rights of the Child.**

You said:

How exactly does the Article 3. of the Convention on the Rights of the Child define the rights of the parents of the child and the duties of the authorities? It is possible that in some situations the alienating parent may be successful to manipulate the authorities to turn against the targeted parent which means situations like that should be examined being just and to guarantee the rights of the parents from the possible arbitrary actions by the authorities.

ChatGPT said:

Article 3 of the UN Convention on the Rights of the Child (UNCRC) and Its Implications for Parental Rights and Authorities' Duties

Article 3 of the **United Nations Convention on the Rights of the Child (UNCRC)** primarily establishes that **the best interests of the child** must be a **primary consideration** in all actions taken by public and private institutions, including **courts, administrative authorities, and social services**. However, it does not explicitly define parental rights in great detail but sets **guidelines** for authorities to act **justly** and avoid arbitrary decisions that could unfairly harm parents.

---

1. Full Text of Article 3 (UNCRC, 1989)

1. **"In all actions concerning children, whether undertaken by public or private social welfare institutions, courts of law, administrative authorities or legislative bodies, the best interests of the child shall be a primary consideration."**
2. **"States Parties undertake to ensure the child such protection and care as is necessary for his or her well-being, taking into account the rights and duties of his or her parents, legal guardians, or other individuals legally responsible for him or her, and, to this end,**

shall take all appropriate legislative and administrative measures."

3. "States Parties shall ensure that the institutions, services, and facilities responsible for the care or protection of children shall conform with the standards established by competent authorities, particularly in the areas of safety, health, and supervision of child care."

---

2. How Article 3 Balances Parental Rights and Authorities' Duties

While the article **prioritizes the best interests of the child**, it also recognizes that:

- Parents **have rights and responsibilities** in raising their children.
- Authorities **must not act arbitrarily** against parents.
- Any intervention must be based on **objective criteria**, not on **manipulation, false accusations, or biased decision-making**.

A) Parental Rights and Responsibilities

📌 **Parents have a natural right to raise their children** unless there is clear evidence of harm.

📌 **Parents must be given the opportunity to be heard** in legal and administrative processes.

📌 **The role of parents is recognized** in ensuring the well-being of their children.

B) Authorities' Duties and Limits

📌 **Authorities must act fairly and impartially**, ensuring **due process** before taking action.

📌 **Intervention is justified only when necessary** to protect the child's well-being.

📌 **Authorities must assess evidence carefully** to avoid wrongful decisions based on manipulation (e.g., false abuse claims, parental alienation tactics).

📌 **States must implement laws to protect parental rights** while ensuring child protection.

---

3. Risks of Authorities Being Manipulated in Parental Alienation Cases

Unfortunately, in **some cases**, an alienating parent may **successfully manipulate** child protection authorities, social workers, or courts by making **false allegations** against the targeted parent. This could lead to:

- **Wrongful restriction of parental rights** (e.g., unfair custody decisions).
- **Unnecessary supervision orders or interventions**.
- **Injustice due to lack of due process** in investigations.

How to Prevent Arbitrary Actions?

✔ **Authorities should require strong, verifiable evidence** before taking action.

✔ **Both parents should have a right to present their case** before decisions are made.

✓ **Independent evaluations** (e.g., psychological assessments, child interviews) should be required.

✓ **Decisions should be reviewed** to correct potential mistakes.

---

4. Conclusion: The Need for Fairness and Just Decision-Making

Article 3 of the UNCRC clearly **protects children's well-being,** but it also **acknowledges parental rights** and **the need for authorities to act fairly.** In cases of **parental alienation,** authorities must be extremely **cautious** not to become tools of manipulation. **A child's best interest should be based on objective facts, not on one parent's influence over the system.**

Would you like more details on how **specific countries** implement these protections?

A comment to the AI´s reply: It is true that **the UN Convention on the Rights of the Child does not mention processes to secure the rights of the parents of the child** but the **Section 2.** needs an **examination** in this matter. **AI mentioned that section in the answer so I will not quote that section** again here directly. **According to that article it guarantees the well-being of the child** it will also **mentions the rights and the duties of the parents of the child. One cannot strip off the rights and the duties of the parents without proving that the actions by the parents of the child are very harmful to the child. Situations like that** always require **a fair trial** and **if someone realizes that he or she is in that kind of situation**

72

then that person should consult with a lawyer specialized in a local family and child law. Regarding this matter **one should also check his or her constitution rights regarding the rule of law and the legal protection provided by the local constitution against the arbitrary actions of the local authorities.**

You said:

What issues should the parent of the child who is the targeted by parental alienation consider when he/she realizes that social work like the child protection authorities have moved to support the parent who is alienating the child? How can the parent who thinks that he/she is being alienated from his/her child can prove their partiality?

ChatGPT said:

How Should a Targeted Parent Respond When Social Services Support the Alienating Parent?

If a **targeted parent** realizes that child protection authorities or social workers **have taken the side of the alienating parent,** they must act carefully, strategically, and legally to **protect their parental rights and the well-being of their child.** Below are **key considerations** and **steps** a targeted parent can take to prove bias and fight against unfair treatment.

---

1. Key Considerations for the Targeted Parent

◆ **Do Not React Emotionally** – While the situation is distressing, **staying calm, rational, and professional** is essential. Emotional reactions can be used against the targeted parent.

◆ **Understand the System's Functioning** – Learn about the **legal framework**, the **child protection system**, and **how decisions are made** in family court and child welfare agencies.

◆ **Know Your Rights** – The targeted parent has **rights to fair treatment, impartial investigation, and to present evidence** in legal and administrative proceedings.

◆ **Gather Strong Evidence** – Alienation cases are difficult to prove, so it is crucial to **document everything**, including communication with social workers, the alienating parent, and the child.

◆ **Prepare for a Long-Term Strategy** – Changing the course of an alienation case **can take time**. The targeted parent should focus on **consistent legal action, documentation, and persistence**.

---

2. How to Prove That Social Services Are Partial?

If the **targeted parent believes that social workers are biased**, they must provide **clear evidence** of partiality. Below are strategies to prove bias:

A) Identify Indicators of Partiality in Social Work

Look for signs that **authorities favor the alienating parent** unfairly:

✓ **Ignoring or downplaying evidence** of alienation.

✓ **Not investigating false allegations** made by the alienating parent.

✓ **Refusing to interview the child properly** or pressuring the child to support one parent.

✓ **Excluding the targeted parent from decision-making processes.**

✓ **Taking action based on allegations rather than facts and evidence.**

B) Collect Documentation and Evidence

The targeted parent should **document everything carefully**:

📌 **Keep records of all interactions with social workers** (emails, reports, meeting summaries).

📌 **Record conversations (if legally allowed in your country).**

📌 **Save copies of court decisions, child welfare assessments, and official correspondence.**

📌 **If the child expresses distress about being manipulated, document their statements.**

📌 **Keep a detailed timeline of alienating behaviors.**

C) Request Access to Case Files and Assessments

Under child protection laws, parents often have the **right to review social services' reports and case files**. The targeted parent should:

✓ Request **all written reports, case notes, and assessments** concerning their case.

✓ Look for **inconsistencies, factual errors, or unfair**

conclusions in reports.
✓ If **false or misleading information** is found, demand corrections and **official responses**.

D) Seek Independent Evaluations

If social workers appear biased, the targeted parent can:
✓ **Request an independent psychological evaluation** of the child and parental relationship.
✓ **Obtain expert opinions** from child psychologists or forensic specialists.
✓ **Ask the court to appoint a neutral evaluator** if needed.

E) Demand Fair Procedures

✓ **Insist on having meetings recorded or documented.**
✓ **Request that a second social worker or independent observer** be present at evaluations.
✓ **Challenge social service decisions in court** if necessary.

---

3. Legal Actions Against Biased Social Services

If **bias is proven**, the targeted parent can take legal steps:

📌 **Appeal Social Service Decisions** – Most countries have procedures for **appealing unfair child protection decisions**.

📌 **File Complaints Against Social Workers** – If misconduct, bias, or professional negligence is found, a complaint can be made to:

- The **child welfare oversight board**
- The **ombudsman**
- A **legal professional association**

➤ **Take the Case to Family Court** – If necessary, a **court order** can force authorities to act fairly and reconsider their stance.

➤ **Media and Advocacy (Carefully Used)** – In some cases, **raising public awareness** or working with **child advocacy organizations** can expose biased practices.

---

4. Conclusion: A Strategic, Evidence-Based Approach Is Necessary

If child protection authorities **wrongly support the alienating parent**, the targeted parent **must act methodically, legally, and persistently** to:
✓ **Prove bias with solid evidence.**
✓ **Demand fair investigations and independent assessments.**
✓ **Use legal appeals and complaints against misconduct.**
✓ **Always focus on the child's best interests** in all arguments and evidence.

Would you like specific **legal references** or strategies based on your country's legal system?

A comment to the AI´s reply: It is most likely a devastating shock for the targeted parent if the child protection authorities will support the alienating parent without having any legal evidence to support their stance in that matter. If

we think the issue from the point of view of the alienating parent that **after he/she has decided to alienate the child from the other parent, it is completely logical for him/her to justify his/her actions and to get the authorities to support him/her. There is no way that this is ethically or morally acceptable, but it is a good idea for the targeted parent to consider this option because it will make his/her life much harder** and **the alienating parent most likely is doing everything to avoid responsibility from his/her actions every way possible.**

You said:

What are the essential international conventions and international treaties and Finnish laws which create obligations to the Finnish authorities regarding the rights of the child and the rights of the parents?

ChatGPT said:

Finland is committed to upholding the rights of children and parents through various international conventions and national laws. These legal instruments establish obligations for Finnish authorities to ensure the welfare of children and respect for parental rights.

International Conventions and Treaties:

1. **United Nations Convention on the Rights of the Child (CRC):**
    - **Adoption:** The CRC was adopted by the UN General Assembly in 1989.

o **Ratification by Finland:** Finland ratified the CRC in 1991, making its provisions legally binding within the country.

lapsiasia.fi

o **Key Obligations:** The CRC mandates that signatory states ensure children's rights to protection, education, health care, and participation in decisions affecting them. It emphasizes that the best interests of the child should be a primary consideration in all actions concerning children.

2. **Hague Convention on the Civil Aspects of International Child Abduction:**
   o **Purpose:** This convention seeks to protect children from international abduction by a parent by establishing procedures to ensure their prompt return to their habitual residence.
   o **Implementation in Finland:** Provisions related to this convention are incorporated into Finnish law, particularly in the Act on Child Custody and Right of Access.

oikeus.fi

Finnish National Laws:

1. **Constitution of Finland:**
   o **Equality and Participation:** The Constitution stipulates that children must be treated equally and as individuals. It ensures their right to

influence matters pertaining to themselves in accordance with their level of development.

oikeusasiamies.fi

2. **Child Welfare Act (417/2007):**
    - ○ **Objective:** This Act aims to protect children's rights to a safe growth environment and balanced development.
    - ○ **Primary Responsibility:** It emphasizes that the primary responsibility for a child's well-being rests with the parents or custodians. Authorities are obligated to intervene when a child's welfare is at risk.

    finlex.fi

3. **Act on Child Custody and Right of Access (361/1983):**
    - ○ **Custody and Access Rights:** This Act outlines the rights and responsibilities of parents regarding child custody and access.
    - ○ **International Provisions:** It includes provisions on international jurisdiction, applicable law, and the recognition and enforcement of foreign decisions concerning child custody and access.

    oikeus.fi

4. **Paternity Act and Maternity Act:**
    - ○ **Parental Determination:** These Acts govern the determination and establishment of paternity and maternity, ensuring a child's right to know and receive care from both parents.

These international and national legal frameworks collectively obligate Finnish authorities to safeguard the rights and welfare of children while respecting and upholding parental rights.

A comment to the AI´s reply: First, **I am from Finland** and **that is why I am using Finland as an example.** International conventions and treaties **vary** between countries, and I recommend that the reader should check **which international conventions and treaties bind his/her country. All those Finnish websites have the English language version. Some of them clearly show the English option** while in the others it is behind **language option Suomi or Suomeksi,** which means **Finnish or in Finnish.**

You said:

If the authorities like the child protection violates the international treaties mentioned earlier and the local laws then can it be interpreted as abetting and inciting to commit crimes if we assume that parental alienation is a crime? It is good to remember that we earlier proved that parental alienation is mental and psychological violence towards both the child and the targeted parent.

ChatGPT said:

The question of whether authorities, such as child protection services, can be considered as *abetting* or *inciting* a crime if they violate international treaties and local laws in cases of parental alienation is complex and depends on several legal factors:

1. Legal Definition of Parental Alienation as a Crime

- In Finland, parental alienation itself is **not explicitly criminalized** as a standalone offense.
- However, if parental alienation involves **psychological violence, coercion, defamation, or child abuse**, it could fall under existing **criminal offenses** such as:
  - *Mental abuse* (Henkinen väkivalta)
  - *Defamation* (Kunnianloukkaus, Rikoslaki 24:9)
  - *Neglect of parental duties* (Laiminlyönti huoltajuustehtävissä)
  - *Abuse of a child* (Lapsen kaltoinkohtelu)

If parental alienation meets the threshold of criminal behavior under Finnish law, then aiding or failing to act against it **could potentially** be examined under criminal liability principles.

2. Authorities' Responsibilities Under Law

Authorities, including child protection services, are bound by:

- **United Nations Convention on the Rights of the Child (CRC)**
- **Finnish Constitution**
- **Child Welfare Act (Lastensuojelulaki, 417/2007)**
- **Act on Child Custody and Right of Access (361/1983)**

These laws require authorities to act **in the best interests of the child** and to remain **impartial** in family disputes. If they take actions that **favor an alienating parent unfairly** or **ignore evidence of alienation**, they could be accused of:

- **Negligence in official duties** (Virkavelvollisuuden laiminlyönti, Rikoslaki 40:9)
- **Discrimination in public office** (Syrjintä virkatehtävässä, Rikoslaki 11:9)
- **Breach of duty** (Virka-aseman väärinkäyttö, Rikoslaki 40:7)

3. Can Authorities Be Accused of Abetting a Crime?

If parental alienation is interpreted as psychological violence or a form of **emotional child abuse**, then:

- Authorities who knowingly **ignore** or **support** the alienation despite evidence **could** be seen as indirectly facilitating harm to the child and the targeted parent.
- In extreme cases, if authorities **actively participate** in alienation (e.g., manipulating reports, favoring one parent unjustly), this **could** be seen as *abetting or inciting harm.*

However, proving that authorities are **intentionally** aiding parental alienation **would be legally challenging,** as most officials act under **bureaucratic procedures** rather than personal intent.

4. Legal Recourse Against Authorities

If a parent believes authorities have acted unfairly in a parental alienation case, they can:

- **File a complaint** with the **Regional State Administrative Agency (AVI)**

- **Appeal** decisions in **Administrative Court (Hallinto-oikeus)**
- **Report suspected official misconduct** to the **Parliamentary Ombudsman or Chancellor of Justice**
- **Seek damages** through **civil lawsuits** if harm can be proven

Conclusion

- If parental alienation is recognized as psychological violence and authorities **actively enable or ignore** it, there **may** be grounds for accusing them of **negligence, abuse of power, or discrimination.**
- However, **proving criminal liability (abetting or incitement)** would require showing that authorities **intentionally** acted to support alienation **against their legal duties**.
- The most effective course of action is to challenge **unfair authority decisions** through **legal appeals and oversight bodies.**

Would you like me to look into legal precedents related to this issue in Finland?

A comment to the AI´s reply: The authorities must know **the international treaties on their own field which their country has ratified** and **the local legislation on their own field**. This principle is derived from **the rule of law**. In **the Finnish Constitution the Section 3. of the Article 2** says that **"The exercise of public powers shall be based on an Act. In all public activity, the law shall be strictly observed."** The **definition of mental and psychological violence** depends on **the local penal code.** In Finland, mental and psychological violence **are criminal acts according to the Finnish Penal Code.** Matters like this **should be consulted with a local lawyer who is specialized with both criminal law,** and **child and family law** before doing any legal actions.

You said:

Is "Lastensuojelun käsikirja" (Eng. The Handbook of Child Protection) by THL (Eng. Finnish Institute for Health and Welfare) a good source evaluating how Finnish child protection authorities do their job legally?

ChatGPT said:

Yes, *Lastensuojelun käsikirja* (The Handbook of Child Protection) by **THL (Finnish Institute for Health and Welfare)** is a **key source** for understanding how Finnish child protection authorities operate within the legal framework. It provides guidance based on:

- **Finnish Child Welfare Act (Lastensuojelulaki 417/2007)**
- **Other relevant national laws** (such as the Constitution, Custody and Right of Access Act, Social Welfare Act)
- **International treaties** (UN Convention on the Rights of the Child, European Human Rights Conventions)

Strengths of THL's Handbook as a Source:

☑ **Official and widely used** – It is an official **government-endorsed** resource for child protection professionals, ensuring it reflects standard practices and legal interpretations.

☑ **Covers legal principles** – It explains **how authorities**

should act, including how they must respect the rights of children and parents.

☑ **Includes practical applications** – It provides **case examples** of how child protection decisions are made in practice.

Limitations of THL's Handbook:

⚠ **Not a legally binding document** – While based on law, it is **not** a law itself but rather an **interpretation and guide** for professionals. Courts may interpret legal matters differently.

⚠ **May reflect institutional bias** – Since it is written **by THL**, which oversees child protection policy, it may **emphasize the authorities' perspective** rather than the concerns of parents critical of the system.

⚠ **Does not replace court decisions** – While it explains how child protection should work, **real-life decisions** are subject to judicial review, administrative appeals, and oversight bodies (like the Parliamentary Ombudsman).

Conclusion:

THL's *Lastensuojelun käsikirja* **is a valuable resource for understanding how Finnish child protection is supposed to function legally.** However, it does **not necessarily reveal potential issues, abuses, or misapplications** of child protection law in individual cases. For critical evaluation, you may also need:

- **Legal case rulings** (Administrative Court & Supreme Administrative Court decisions)
- **Parliamentary Ombudsman reports** (Eduskunnan oikeusasiamiehen ratkaisut)

- **Independent legal analyses** (academic research, expert opinions)

Would you like assistance in finding alternative sources or legal cases relevant to child protection authority decisions?

A comment to the AI´s reply: The THL´s handbook is to show how **the child protection of Finland should work,** and **I have not found the translation of this book in English**. However, modern AI applications **can translate this book** to other languages quite easily if necessary. **The reason why I made this question to AI** was to show the readers that **there might be handbooks in various countries** which explain **how the child protection authorities work** and to give the **readers a chance to compare the handbooks and the actions of the child protection in their cases**. Hopefully this will help readers **to understand how the child protection authorities should work.** Like the AI said handbooks like this **are not the only legal sources** in legal cases involving **children, child protection**, and they should be used **together with local laws and the local legal practice**.

After we have examined parental alienation and the possibility that **the alienating parent has manipulated the authorities to support him/her** then we should examine **the legal dimension of parental alienation a bit.** It should be mentioned that **the targeted parent has felt both emotional and legal costs of the parental alienation.** It is possible **that the parental alienation could have been quite expensive for him/her because of the costs of the possible legal cases. Luckily most of the parents of the child divorce or separate without any lawsuits.** According to the THL (Eng. Finnish Institute for Health and Welfare) article**"Vaativat erotilanteet and eron jälkeinen väkivalta"** (Eng. **Demanding separations and the post-separation violence)** about **90 % of divorces and separations of the parents of the child happen without any lawsuits.** In this kind of **complicated legal issues, it is always wise to consult a local lawyer specialized in the crime law and the child and family law.**

You said:

Even though parental alienation has not been criminalized in the Finnish Penal Code it should be noted that parental alienation is mental and psychological violence which may be a crime of assault or aggravated assault according the the Chapter 21´s Sections 5 and 6 of Finnish Penal Code. In the Finnish Penal Code attempting to do assault or aggravated assault is punishable. One of the most important human rights is the right to have family life which in the authorities cannot violate arbitrarily and this supports the hard line towards any arbitrary actions by the authorities.

ChatGPT said:

You make an important argument based on **both criminal law and human rights principles**. While **parental alienation** is not explicitly criminalized in the **Finnish Penal Code**, it can still fall under certain legal provisions, particularly **assault-related offenses** and **human rights protections**.

---

1. Parental Alienation as Psychological Violence (Assault & Aggravated Assault)

The **Finnish Penal Code (Rikoslaki, 39/1889)** defines both **assault** (*pahoinpitely*) and **aggravated assault** (*törkeä pahoinpitely*) in **Chapter 21 (Crimes Against Life and Health):**

- **Section 5 – Assault (Pahoinpitely)**
  - Covers both **physical** and **mental/psychological violence** that causes pain, suffering, or harm to health.
  - Psychological abuse that leads to **serious emotional distress or mental health issues** (e.g., depression, anxiety) could be considered under this section.
- **Section 6 – Aggravated Assault (Törkeä pahoinpitely)**
  - If the act causes **serious injury, permanent health damage, or significant suffering**, it may qualify as aggravated assault.

- o If parental alienation results in **self-harm, suicide risk, or long-term psychological trauma**, it could be **interpreted as aggravated assault**.
- **Section 15 – Attempting Assault is Punishable**
  - o Even an **attempt** to commit assault or aggravated assault is **criminally punishable** under Finnish law.

👉 **Legal Implication:**

If parental alienation is proven to cause **severe psychological harm**, it could be prosecuted as **assault** or **aggravated assault**, depending on the severity of the mental suffering inflicted on the targeted parent or child.

---

2. Violation of the Right to Family Life (Human Rights)

The right to family life is **protected under both Finnish law and international human rights treaties.**

- **Finnish Constitution (Perustuslaki, 731/1999), Section 10**
  - o Ensures the protection of private and family life.
  - o Arbitrary interference by authorities may **violate constitutional rights**.
- **European Convention on Human Rights (ECHR), Article 8**
  - o Protects the right to **respect for private and family life**.

- The **state (including child protection authorities)** must not arbitrarily separate families without strong legal grounds.
- **UN Convention on the Rights of the Child (CRC), Article 9**
  - States must ensure that children are **not separated from their parents unless it is in the child's best interest.**
  - Children have the right to **maintain contact with both parents** unless there are serious safety concerns.

👉 **Legal Implication:**
If authorities **support parental alienation without justification,** it could be considered a **violation of human rights** and **potentially an abuse of power** (*virkarikos*).

---

3. Arbitrary Actions by Authorities

If child protection authorities or other officials **actively or negligently support parental alienation**, their actions could be interpreted as:

- **Abuse of public office (Virkavelvollisuuden rikkominen, RL 40:9)**
  - If a public official knowingly **violates laws or obligations,** leading to harm.
- **Discrimination in public office (RL 11:9)**
  - If authorities **favor one parent unjustly,** leading to a violation of the other parent's rights.

91

☞ **Legal Implication:**
If authorities **act unjustly**, their actions should be challenged in **Administrative Court (Hallinto-oikeus)** or **reported to the Parliamentary Ombudsman (Eduskunnan oikeusasiamies).**

Conclusion

Parental alienation, while not directly criminalized, **can still be prosecuted under Finnish law** if it leads to **psychological violence (assault)** or **violates fundamental rights (family life, due process).** Authorities must act **impartially** and **not support alienation,** or they could be **legally accountable** for human rights violations or official misconduct.

Would you like **case law examples** or **legal interpretations** related to this?

A comment to the AI´s reply: This is only **what Finnish laws say about this issue** and **laws in different countries vary.** It is true that **parental alienation is not criminalized in the Finnish Penal Code,** but it can be seen as **mental or psychological violence** towards **the targeted parent and his/her children.** That kind of violence **may have long-term consequences** on **that parent and his/her children.** It should be mentioned that **attempting assault or aggravated assault are both punishable according to the Finnish Penal Code.** If someone **wants to sue the other parent** in a case like this **then he/she should first consult with a local lawyer who is specialized in both local crime law and local child and family law.**

You said:

How smart is it using the Finnish Penal Code to define mental and psychological violence both through actions and the consequences of these actions?

ChatGPT said:

Using the **Finnish Penal Code (Rikoslaki, 39/1889)** to define **mental and psychological violence** through both **actions and their consequences** is legally and logically **a strong approach** for several reasons:

---

1. The Finnish Penal Code Already Recognizes Psychological Violence

- **Chapter 21 (Crimes Against Life and Health)** explicitly includes **mental violence** as a form of **assault (pahoinpitely).**
- The law does not limit violence to physical harm—**psychological abuse** causing **emotional distress, depression, or anxiety** is legally recognized.

Relevant Sections:

- **Section 5 – Assault (Pahoinpitely)**
  - Covers **both physical and psychological harm** if it causes **pain or suffering**.
  - The law does not require direct physical violence—**mental abuse** qualifies if it damages the victim's well-being.

- **Section 6 – Aggravated Assault (Törkeä pahoinpitely)**
  - If the **mental harm is severe** (e.g., leads to **self-harm, suicide attempts, PTSD**), the offense may be classified as **aggravated**.
- **Section 15 – Attempting Assault is Punishable**
  - If someone **intentionally** engages in actions likely to **cause psychological harm**, even if the harm is not fully realized, they can still be prosecuted.

👉 **Smart Strategy:**
Using these sections allows courts to **evaluate parental alienation case-by-case** based on **the severity of harm suffered**, rather than requiring a new, separate law.

---

2. The Law Focuses on Consequences, Not Just Intent

The Finnish legal system **does not require proof of intent to harm**—if the **actions result in significant suffering**, they may still be criminal.

- **For example:**
  - If an alienating parent **systematically manipulates a child** into **hating the other parent**, causing the targeted parent **severe depression** → it could be **classified as psychological assault**.
  - If this leads to **suicidal thoughts or self-harm**, it might qualify as **aggravated assault**.

94

☝ **Smart Strategy:**
This approach **focuses on the real impact on victims**, not just whether the perpetrator claims "good intentions."

---

3. International Human Rights Law Supports This Interpretation

- **European Convention on Human Rights (ECHR), Article 3:**
    - Prohibits **torture and inhuman or degrading treatment**—which can include **severe psychological abuse.**
- **United Nations Convention on the Rights of the Child (CRC), Article 19:**
    - Requires states to protect children from **"all forms of mental violence".**
- **Finnish Constitution, Section 7:**
    - Protects personal integrity—including **mental well-being.**

☝ **Smart Strategy:**
This interpretation **aligns with international human rights obligations**, making it harder for authorities to ignore.

---

4. Allows Holding Authorities Accountable

If **child protection authorities** or **family courts** fail to act against **mental violence** (e.g., parental alienation), they may be guilty of:

- **Negligence in office (RL 40:10 – Virkavelvollisuuden rikkominen)**
- **Discrimination in office (RL 11:9 – Syrjintä virkatoiminnassa)**
  - If they favor one parent arbitrarily and **ignore psychological harm** inflicted on the child or the other parent.

👉 **Smart Strategy:**
Using this legal framework allows affected parents to **demand accountability from authorities** through legal complaints.

Conclusion: Why This is a Smart Legal Strategy

☑ **Already part of existing law** – No need to wait for new legislation.
☑ **Recognizes real psychological harm** – Even without physical violence.
☑ **Aligns with international law** – Strengthens the legal argument.
☑ **Can be used to challenge biased authorities** – Ensures justice.

Would you like to see **court precedents** where psychological violence has been prosecuted in Finland or the EU?

A comment to the AI´s reply: Like the AI said it is **smart to define mental and psychological violence both through actions and consequences. Doing mental and psychological violence shows that the perpetrator who is doing so either**

intentionally or through his/her disregard violates the law when **the consequences of these actions are very important evaluating the seriousness of these actions in the big picture**.

You said:

What kind of advice would ChatGPT give to a targeted parent in a parental alienation case for court cases regarding the guardianship, alimony and meeting rights of his/her children?

ChatGPT said:

A **targeted parent** in a **parental alienation case** should approach court proceedings **strategically and legally,** ensuring that they provide **strong evidence, well-prepared arguments, and legal support**. Below is **detailed advice** regarding **guardianship (custody), alimony (child support), and visitation rights** in Finnish family law.

---

1. Guardianship (Custody) – "Huoltajuus"

Key Legal Framework in Finland:

- **Child Custody and Right of Access Act (Laki lapsen huollosta ja tapaamisoikeudesta 361/1983)**
- **Convention on the Rights of the Child (CRC)**
- **European Convention on Human Rights (ECHR)**

Legal Strategy for Guardianship Cases

A. Proving That You Are a Fit and Involved Parent

☑ Show that you have **consistently taken care of your child's needs**, including:

- Providing financial and emotional support.
- Actively participating in **education, healthcare, and extracurricular activities**.
- Having a stable home environment.

☑ Present **evidence of parental alienation**:

- **Messages, emails, or recordings** showing the other parent **discouraging contact**.
- **Witness statements** from teachers, psychologists, or family friends.
- **Child's reactions** (e.g., if the child suddenly rejects you without any valid reason).

☑ **Request psychological evaluations**:

- If parental alienation is suspected, the court can order **psychological or social worker assessments** to determine if the child has been manipulated.

B. Fighting for Sole or Joint Custody

👉 **Best Outcome: Joint custody** unless extreme circumstances (e.g., abuse) exist.
👉 **Worst Outcome:** The alienating parent gets sole custody and further restricts contact.

☑ **Argue for joint custody**, emphasizing:

- The child benefits from having both parents in their life.
- The alienating parent has acted **against the child's best interest** by cutting contact.
- The court should **not reward the alienating parent's behavior** with sole custody.

⚠ **Extreme Cases:** If the alienating parent is causing severe psychological harm, **request sole custody** based on the child's best interest.

---

2. Alimony (Child Support) – "Elatusmaksu"

Legal Strategy for Fair Child Support

☑ **Ensure that financial obligations are fair:**

- Child support should be **based on real income** and **shared responsibilities**.
- If the alienating parent **prevents contact**, you can argue that child support should be **adjusted** to reflect your limited parental role.

☑ **Legal Arguments:**

- **If the alienating parent is wealthier**, argue for a **fair contribution split**.

- If you **lose visitation rights unfairly**, ask the court to **reduce payments** since you're being treated unfairly as a parent.

⚠ **Beware:** The alienating parent may try to **maximize financial gains** while **blocking visitation**.

---

3. Meeting Rights (Visitation) – "Tapaamisoikeus"

Legal Strategy to Secure Your Rights

A. Fight for Maximum Visitation Time

☑ **Standard legal principle:**

- **Children have the right to maintain relationships with both parents** unless serious risk exists.

☑ **Request frequent, uninterrupted visits:**

- If the child lives with the alienating parent, push for **overnight stays** and **holiday visits**.
- If the alienating parent has **severely influenced the child**, ask the court for **supervised visits** to gradually rebuild trust.

B. Handling Alienating Parent's Excuses

⚠ The alienating parent may claim:

✖ "The child doesn't want to see you."

☑ **Counter-argument**: The child's opinion has been **manipulated** and should be **evaluated professionally**.

✖ "You are unfit to be a parent."

☑ **Counter-argument**: Provide evidence of **your stable lifestyle, care, and previous relationship with the child**.

✖ "The child is too busy."

☑ **Counter-argument**: The law prioritizes **parental relationships over hobbies**.

C. Request Court-Ordered Support

If the alienating parent **continues to block contact**, request:

- **Fines or penalties** for non-compliance.
- **Court-supervised transfers of the child** to prevent excuses.
- **Therapeutic intervention** to help rebuild the child-parent bond.

---

4. Gathering Strong Evidence

☑ **Maintain records of:**

- **Missed visitation attempts** (texts, emails, witnesses).
- **Negative comments made by the other parent** about you.
- **Attempts to stay in contact** (messages, calls).

✅ **Get expert reports** from:

- Child psychologists
- Teachers
- Family therapists

✅ **Engage a good lawyer** who specializes in family law.

Final Strategic Advice

1. **Stay calm and professional** – Do not show frustration in court.
2. **Always act in the child's best interest** – Courts favor parents who focus on the child's well-being.
3. **Use legal means to fight for your rights** – Don't escalate conflicts outside the legal process.

Would you like help drafting **a legal argument or court submission**?

A comment to the AI´s reply: The advice given by ChatGPT looks very good. It must be **very frustrating, mentally stressing and economically expensive** for the targeted parent **to fight in the court issues regarding the child like guardianship, alimony and meeting rights**. In those matters **it would be wiser for both parents try make some concessions in matters**

regarding the child and try to see the issues also from the point of view of the other parent in the name of the best interest of the child. There is an old saying that **a slim peace better than a fat argument** meaning that **a slightly unfavourable peace is better than fat argument because that kind of peace will bring stability to the situation.** That kind of peace requires **both sides to make concessions.** It is **difficult to evaluate the long-term consequences to the children and their relations to the parents. The worst-case scenario for the alienating parent is that the parental alienation fails** and **when the children are adults, they will know all relevant issues the alienating parent** who tried to make them **to lose not only their other parent but also the entire family of that parent.**

You said:

Does those previous advice also help in the other countries because they might have different laws and legal systems?

ChatGPT said:

Yes, the advice I gave is broadly useful in **many countries,** but legal systems **differ** significantly based on national laws, legal traditions, and judicial discretion. Below is how the advice might apply in **different legal systems:**

---

1. How Legal Systems Affect Parental Alienation Cases

A. Common Law Countries (e.g., USA, UK, Canada, Australia)

☑ **Court decisions (precedents) matter**: Judges rely on previous cases. If a similar case ruled against alienation, it can **help your case.**

☑ **Parental alienation might be explicitly recognized**: Some states (e.g., **Brazil, Italy, parts of the USA**) have laws defining parental alienation as **harmful to children.**

☑ **Psychological evaluations play a major role**: Courts often require expert reports to determine alienation's impact.

◆ **Key Challenge:** Courts tend to favor **stability**—if the child has lived with the alienating parent for years, it may be hard to reverse custody.

B. Civil Law Countries (e.g., Finland, Germany, France, Spain)

☑ **Strict statutory law**: Courts focus on **written laws rather than past cases.** You must reference **family law codes and human rights treaties.**

☑ **State authorities may be involved**: Social workers and child protection agencies have **stronger roles**, which means proving **their neutrality** is essential.

◆ **Key Challenge:** If social services **support** the alienating parent, it can be hard to change their stance without solid evidence.

C. Religious and Customary Law Countries (e.g., some Middle Eastern & Asian countries)

☑ **Parental roles may be more traditional:** Fathers often get custody in Islamic law, while in some Asian cultures, **maternal custody is prioritized.**

☑ **Courts may favor local customs over international treaties:** The **UN Convention on the Rights of the Child (CRC)** may have limited enforcement.

◆ **Key Challenge:** If parental alienation **isn't legally recognized**, proving harm to the child can be more difficult.

---

2. Key International Conventions That Apply Everywhere

Even though each country has its own laws, the following **international treaties** influence court decisions **globally:**

◆ **UN Convention on the Rights of the Child (CRC)** – Protects the child's right to maintain contact with both parents.

◆ **European Convention on Human Rights (ECHR)** – Guarantees the **right to family life** (Article 8).

◆ **The Hague Convention on Parental Abduction** – Helps recover children illegally removed across borders.

These treaties can be **powerful legal arguments** if local laws **do not explicitly protect against parental alienation**.

---

3. Adjusting the Strategy for Different Countries

- **USA** – Emphasize **psychological harm** to the child. Courts rely on expert testimony.
- **UK** – Courts prioritize **child's best interest**. Mediation is encouraged.
- **Germany** – Family courts work **closely with social services**, so challenge their neutrality **carefully**.
- **France** – Judges focus on **parental cooperation**. If you prove the alienating parent is uncooperative, it helps your case.
- **Nordic Countries (Finland, Sweden, Norway)** – Child protection authorities **play a major role**. Psychological evaluations are crucial.

---

4. Best Universal Legal Approach

- ☑ **Document evidence of alienation** (messages, expert opinions).
- ☑ **Cite international treaties if local laws are weak**.
- ☑ **Avoid aggressive legal battles**—courts favor **cooperative parents**.
- ☑ **Request psychological assessments** to prove alienation's effect.

Would you like help adapting the legal argument for a **specific country**?

A comment to the AI´s reply: I asked this question because **the earlier parts of this book were very heavily based on Finland and the Finnish laws.** Since this book is in English, **I wanted to provide the reader some information how different countries handle parental alienation cases in practice.**

Conclusion

At **the beginning of the Conclusion,** we can use **AI to summarize the discussion** which we had in **a single ChatGPT thread.**

You said:

Can you make a short summary on the discussion in this thread?

ChatGPT said:

Sure! Here's a **short summary** of our discussion:

1. **Parental Alienation & Its Consequences** – We explored how parental alienation is a form of **mental and psychological violence** that can have severe effects on both the targeted parent and the child. In extreme cases, it may contribute to **family tragedies** (though rare) and increase the risk of **suicide** for alienated parents.
2. **Legal & Human Rights Perspective** – While Finland and many other countries **haven't criminalized parental alienation**, it can still be considered **assault or aggravated assault** under **Chapter 21, Sections 5 & 6 of the Finnish Penal Code**. Additionally, international treaties such as the **UN Convention on the Rights of the Child (CRC)** and the **European Convention on Human Rights (ECHR)** establish obligations for authorities to protect family bonds.
3. **Role of Authorities & Potential Bias** – Child protection authorities sometimes **side with the alienating parent**, either due to manipulation or systemic bias. This raises concerns about **justice and neutrality** in handling

custody disputes. The Finnish **"Lastensuojelun käsikirja" (Handbook of Child Protection)** by THL is a key document explaining child protection processes.

4. **Legal Strategy for Targeted Parents** – Parents facing alienation should:
    - **Gather strong evidence** (messages, psychological evaluations).
    - **Challenge biased authority actions** using Finnish and international laws.
    - **Seek expert testimony** to highlight the **harm** of alienation.
    - **Ensure courts focus on the child's best interests** while emphasizing the right to family life.

5. **Application in Different Legal Systems** – While the **core legal arguments** apply in many countries, the approach varies based on whether the system is **common law, civil law, or religious law**. Some nations, like **Brazil and Italy,** explicitly recognize **parental alienation** in their laws, while others rely on general child welfare principles.

Would you like a more **detailed version** of any part?

A comment on the summary made by AI: I think that the summary made by AI is **very good**. It is a great pleasure to see how **AI found the most important issues from the discussion**. When talking about parental alienation **this gives hope** that **AI is most likely very useful tool evaluating parental alienation**. Probably **the greatest problem regarding people evaluating parental alienation** is the fact that **the person who made the evaluation may be more likely support the evaluation** than **to**

change it even if there are very good reasons to change the evaluation.

The purpose of this book is to help the people who experience parental alienation to use AI like ChatGPT to acquire information about parental alienation and to gain advice how to react on against parental alienation. Another theme of the book is to start discussion how to use AI against parental alienation. The questions which I made in the book are example questions. I encourage people who read this book to make their own questions to AI because the person who experiences parental alienation is the best expert in his/her own matter to discuss with AI in that matter and to make questions to AI which are custom-tailored to fulfil his/her needs.

Regarding AI it should be remembered that AI is a tool and no more than an unofficial advisor. In all legal matters regarding parental alienation, one should consult with a lawyer who is at least specialized in local child and family law and if the matter is about a possible crime, then that lawyer should be specialized also in crime law. Any information provided by AI should be checked from the independent sources if someone plans to use that information officially. Regarding AI it is very important that the person who is experiencing parental alienation should by his/her own work to gain sufficient knowledge that he/she can ask AI questions which are extensive enough and later use more exact questions which are designed to get from AI the answers to the questions from the answers of the first questions.

I want that the reader of this book will remember couple of issues from this book. The first issue is that the modern AI chats are a very innovation, and it is very likely that they will develop a lot during the following years. It seems to be likely that they will offer even help in the future because of the expected development. The second issue is that they are not problem-solving silver bullets, but they are as good as people who designed their AI models, the training data they used, and the questions asked from them are. The third issue is that in real life situations it is probably wiser approach to ask the same questions from several AI chats than just trust one of them regardless how good that one is. The idea is to compare answers given by these AI chats.